SIDELIGHTS

SIDELIGHTS

ON NEW LONDON AND
NEWER YORK

AND OTHER ESSAYS

By

G. K. CHESTERTON

Essay Index Reprint Series

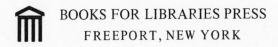

BOOKS FOR LIBRARIES PRESS
FREEPORT, NEW YORK

First Published 1932
Reprinted 1968

LIBRARY OF CONGRESS CATALOG CARD NUMBER:
68-8447

PRINTED IN THE UNITED STATES OF AMERICA

A FIRST WORD

LOOSE as it is, there is a link between these light essays; or at least between the two principal groups of them. In these two cases I am dealing with two different things, in the sense of things that are bound to be different from myself. They are both alien as the term is applied to a stranger from a strange land; though not necessarily as it is applied to an undesirable alien. One is divided from me in time and the other in space. One is the New World, in the sense of the new generation, with all the new fashions and fantasies which 'Youth' is supposed to have precipitated into the post-war Society. The other is the New World in an older sense; the western world that we call America, and the New Race which some believe to be springing up there. And though the notes I have made on both novelties are in themselves very scrappy and disproportionate, they observe throughout one particular line and limit, and work to one particular end.

I have observed that some are rather nervous when writing about Youth; and, perhaps for the same reason, rather nervous about writing about America. This results in shocking exhibitions of mildness and tact; and the failure to condemn things that really ought to be condemned. On the other hand, I have seen all the good effects of this deplorable amiability spoilt by something else, that is quite consistent with amiability; and that is arrogance. I mean that the critic is really disliked, not because he treats wrong things as wrong, or even as exceptionally wrong; but because he treats himself as exceptionally right. I have therefore been very careful in this book to indulge in vulgar abuse, of the heartiest description; but not to indulge in what seems to me much more vulgar; what is now called optimism and what used to be called vanity.

I mean seriously that this distinction is of great importance in dealing with new or strange things; with the young or with the foreigner. It is perfectly lawful for me to say that I think Gate-Crashing a good deal less honest than house-breaking. What is not lawful for me is to pretend, as too many of the traditional school have pretended, that the old Victorian villa was a perfectly ideal house. I have therefore devoted a whole chapter to the destruction of that myth; and to bringing more than its gates to the ground in the crash. Similarly, it is my right, as well as my pleasure, to say that Prohibition is as nonsensical as compulsory nakedness; or any other form of barbarism enforced by violence. But though I have a right to be violent about that violence, I have not got a right to talk as if I were superior to all such problems merely because I am an Englishman; or to deny the responsibility of England for originating the Manichæan madness that is called Puritanism. It is my duty to ask myself, in a spirit of Christian humility, whether, if England ever did produce so many stupid and provincial Prohibitionists, she could also produce so many gallant and adventurous Bootleggers. I hope she would never make such a law; but could she break such a law; so vigorously; so democratically; on so vast a scale? I am here to recommend self-examination and searchings of heart. Anyhow I am here to protest against superiority as a primary principle of criticism. In judging the Rising Generation, in judging the New World, I have tried to avoid the least suggestion that the judge himself is not in danger of the judgment.

In this connection, there might appear something like a rather too sublime survey of the whole world, in the title which opens the last section, consisting of a few literary essays on lines somewhat similar to the rest. May I explain that I should not normally, being of sound mind, give an article the universal and devastating title of "The Spirit of the Age in Literature"; nor write it in the somewhat simple and didactic style in which it is written. The truth is that it was one of a series, mostly to be written by men much more educational than myself; "The Spirit of the Age in Science," "The Spirit of the Age in Politics," and so on. I do not often indulge in education; and I trust my brief outbreak may be forgiven.

CONTENTS

CONTENTS

PART III

OTHER ESSAYS

PART I

NEW LONDON

I. ON BRIGHT OLD THINGS—AND OTHER THINGS

WHAT embitters the world is not excess of criticism, but absence of self-criticism. It is comparatively of little consequence that you occasionally break out and abuse other people, so long as you do not absolve yourself. The former is a natural collapse of human weakness; the latter is a blasphemous assumption of divine power. And in the modern world, where everybody is quarrelling about the urgent necessity of peace, nobody notices how this notion has really poisoned the relations of nations and men. Thus the Irishman would never have minded the English saying he was mad; or even that he was murderous and slanderous and cruel. There was something to be said for the assertion; and Irishmen were often ready, if not to admit it about themselves, at least to admit it about each other. The trouble began when the Englishman advanced the obviously ludicrous proposition that he himself was sane; that he was practical and sensible and well-balanced. No wonder a whole nation went wild at so fantastic a fancy as that. What the Prussian said about the French or the other Latins was simply ignorance: the ignorance found only among the seriously educated. It was what the

Prussian said about the Prussian, that made half the world smell afar off something that stank with spiritual pride. The moral is the same about much milder and more amiable things; indeed it is rather specially true about mild and amiable things. The trouble with the philanthropist is not that he does not love all men moderately, but rather that he generally loves one man too well. And, contemplating the sort of philanthropist who is also an egoist, I am tempted to recommend him to try being a man-hater, that men may more easily love him. I am tempted to say to him: hate men as a sort of holiday; beat and kick them for a reasonable interval; burn down their houses, in moderation, and lay waste all civilization within reasonable limits. But do not be kind merely to exhibit your own kindness; for that is an insult that is never forgiven. When you are helping people, pray for a spirit of humility; I had almost said, when you are helping them, pray for an appearance of helplessness. The deadly word "patronage" is, like so many such, a word that has decayed from a much nobler meaning. But in this sense we may find another significance in the old conception of patron saints. It may mean that a man has jolly well got to be a saint, before he ventures to be a patron.

Now this is the first thing to note in all the fuss about modern fashion; about Jazz and Cocktails and Bright Young Things. In all the talk on both sides,

-〔4〕-

hardly anybody has attempted what I am going to attempt here—a criticism by some standard other than the habits of the critic; a judgment that is not merely a justification of the judge. We all know the kind of judge or police magistrate who does say complacently about some educational or domestic problem, "Well, I was treated like that" or, "I myself went to that sort of school." And in the awful silence that follows, every prisoner, policeman and spectator resists the overpowering impulse to point dramatically and say, "And behold the deplorable result!" In short, the trouble arises from the aged merely praising their own age; just as the rising generation is only praising its own generation. Neither is of the slightest value as judgment, for both are only blowing their own trumpets; and the great Trumpeter is silent.

There are two kinds of old gentlemen who generally write on this subject. Perhaps the more common (in every sense of the word) is the old gentleman who praises the young people, in order to prove that he is really a young gentleman. He will show everybody that he also is a bright young thing; and we need not now inquire how many are bright enough to think him a silly old goat. The other type of man does not pretend to be youthful, but he does judge everything youthful by the fashions of his own youth. I think him the more respectable because the more realistic of the two. But he is not realistic enough; because he does not realistically criticize his own youth and his own type or class or epoch; or, in effect, himself. He is always talking about vanished simplicities, or supposed simplicities, which "were good enough for him." It seldom occurs to him to ask whether he was good enough for them.

Now it is easy to fall into either of these follies; and I also appear here only in the humble capacity of an old fool. But I propose, even in my second childhood, to be the sort of fool who seeks after wisdom; and what I wish to do here is to establish some sort of standard which shall be related to the wisdom of the ages, and not to the quarrel of the generations. I would try to remove these things from the test of time, and subject them to the test of truth. It is not merely a question of what old people did when they were young; it is quite as much a question of what young people will do when they are old enough to know better. The ideal is quite as likely to be in the future as in the past; only it is silly to suppose that it must be in the present. But the point is that when the critic calls the present good or bad, he ought to be comparing it with the ideal and not with the rather dismal reality called himself.

Next, we may note that both these old gentlemen are sentimentalists; but rather especially the young old gentleman, who so often accuses the old-fashioned old gentleman of sentiment. There is much more of mere gush in the person who excites himself about the Woman with a Future than in the person who rather prides himself on being a Man with a Past. For the one old fool is swept off his feet by the mere sight of youth from the outside; the other at least by the experience of youth from the inside. The other may be a bore with a tendency to moralize; but it is not quite so much of a bore as the tendency to immoralize; or to moralize against morality. It is not easy to find a worse bore than the Bright Old Thing when he actually trots about grinning and congratulating people on being divorced, as the other used to congratulate them on being married. His argument has the very soul of monotony because it is the essence of tautology. It consists entirely of saying that Polyanna is a modern girl, and therefore believes in modern ideas of dress or drink or general behaviour. Which is about as intellectually helpful as saying that Pongo is a monkey and therefore eats like a monkey and drinks like a monkey, and gives (on the whole) a very good imitation of a monkey. It does not even begin an intelligent inquiry about whether it is best for us to be monkeys or to be modern. Sometimes he sinks to the senile depth of saying that vows belonged to the Victorian age, or that constancy went out with crinolines. Which is about as logical as saying that the multiplication table was made of mahogany, or that the mathematical idea of triangles went out with three-cornered hats. But we need no longer poke about in the dregs and sediment of the poor old sentimentalist's mind. The point is that he is quite as unintellectual, in his notion of the New Morality, as the very stupidest of the other sort could ever have been in his defence of the Old Morality. The other old gentleman (who is often a rather better educated old gentleman) may have an alarming tendency to say suddenly *O tempora O mores*. But both are only thinking about the times and neither is really thinking about the morals.

This is what is missed both by the Bright Old Thing and the Dull Old Thing, who is sometimes sufficiently preferable to be called the Dear Old Thing: that it is possible for an independent mind to criticize many recent social changes, quite without any question of sentimentalism, and sometimes without any question of morality. They can be judged as we judge any historic changes in manners and in the arts of life; and they may be quite impartially condemned, as we condemn any old historic decline in those manners or those arts. We can give impersonal reasons for our criticisms or condemnation, just as we give impersonal reasons for thinking the Silver Age less than the Golden Age or the Spain of the eighteenth century less than the Spain of the sixteenth. That is quite different from the petty

-{8}-

personal matter of proving the England of the twentieth century less than the England of the nineteenth, merely because some of us happened to be born in the nineteenth. I was not born in the time of Charles the First any more than in the time of Charles the Second. But that does not prevent me from thinking that the dress and demeanour of a Cavalier by Van Dyck is both nobler and more natural than that of a courtier by Kneller. I try to judge it by standards of eternal common sense, as I should judge ancient Greeks or Egyptians. That is the kind of criticism of the new fads or fashions which is really needed. That is the kind of criticism that is entirely neglected. And that kind of criticism is so much neglected, that I have been driven, in my last doddering or dying moments, to do it myself.

I propose in these few essays to deal in turn with some of these fashions, which everybody is talking about and nobody is thinking about. I propose to compare the Modern Girl not with the Old Girl but with the Girl; not to contrast her with Queen Victoria but with Venus Verticordia and immortal Beauty. I propose to compare modern dancing, not with the polka as performed by Lord Palmerston, but with the ancient ritual of the Dance, as probably performed by Adam and Eve. If I should be so unwise as to say anything about bobbing or shingling, it would not be to contrast it with the ringlets of Miss Letitia Landon, but to contrast it with the more or less recognizable institution of Hair; which was worn without either expedient by Eve or Lady Godiva. While doing justice to what I think excellent in many modern expedients, I would suggest that several of the expedients do not answer even their own purpose of expediency. I think, for instance, that the time has come when advertisement should be criticized. So far, advertisement has only been advertised. I should like to point out that what is called Publicity is often the very opposite of making things public. I should like to point out that this age, which is chattering about Psychoanalysis, is entirely neglecting elementary Psychology. But I write this preface only to insist on one point; that I do not criticize Jazz because I am an exquisitely elegant waltzer; or attempt to regulate the fashions because I regard myself as an eternal fashion-plate. On these points I can call on many witnesses to clear my character.

II. ON CALLING NAMES—CHRISTIAN AND OTHERWISE

It is said that there has been a moral breakdown; but let us be comforted; it is only a mental breakdown. Indeed I only call it a breakdown, because that was the name of a nigger dance. But it is not so much like the breakdown as it is like the cake-walk. And the case against the cake-walk is that it claims to be one in which you can eat your cake and have it. In other words, the real objection to much of modern fashion is an objection based on reason, and not specially on morality. In certain respects (not all or even perhaps most), current culture seems to me to have simply fallen to a lower level of civilization and to be now a little nearer to niggers or even to monkeys.

I will take one example of what I mean, precisely because it has nothing directly to do with morality at all. It is now the custom of most young people to shout at each other by their Christian names, or the abbreviations of their Christian names, or the most intimate substitutes for their Christian names, as soon as they know each other, or before they know each other. If (as you and I and all smart people are aware) the dashing and distinguished Miss Vernon-Vavasour was

known in baptism as Gloria but among her most devoted friends as Gurgles, there is now no difference between those who call her Gurgles and those who
call her Glory and those who would normally prefer,
when suddenly presented to somebody they do not
know from Eve, to call her Miss Vernon-Vavasour.
As soon as she is seen as a distant dot on the other
side of the tennis court, a total stranger will yell at her
as Gurgles, because he hears a crowd of other total
strangers doing the same. He will use her nickname,
because he has never known enough about her to have
heard her name. Or he will use the first name, because
he has not been in her company for a sufficient number
of seconds to get as far as the last one.

Now all this has nothing directly to do with right
and wrong. I suppose there are savage tribes in which a
person only possesses one name, and so has to be addressed by it. It might be maintained that the first name
is always the noblest and most sacred in a religious and
moral sense. Perhaps the Bright Young Things only
use Christian names to express their holy zeal for anything that is Christian. Perhaps they talk of Tom only
to remind him of his solemn dedication to St. Thomas
of Canterbury or St. Thomas Aquinas. Perhaps they
shriek at Peter to thrill him with the thought that he
is the rock on which the Church is built. Perhaps they
compress into the loud and sometimes peremptory cry

of "Jack!" all the mingled mysteries of St. John the Baptist and St. John the Evangelist. Perhaps, on the other hand, they don't. But anyhow, it is quite true that Tom, Dick and Harry are the names of saints; while Jones, Brown and Robinson are often only the names of snobs. Therefore the practice of talking about Tom, Dick and Harry instead of about Mr. Jones, Mr. Brown and Mr. Robinson, might be adopted for many reasons, noble and ignoble, worldly and unworldly. I complain of it here, not because it is worldly, but on the contrary, because it shows a lack of appreciation of the world. It especially shows a lack of appreciation of the civilized world. It shows a dullness in distinguishing and tasting the arts of civilization.

Anyhow, the matter of Christian names does not it-self involve Christian morals. To take another alternative possibility; some of those happy Utopias described by Mr. Wells might possibly abolish all Christian names, or even abolish all names. It might entirely deprive us of names and only provide us with numbers. We might have labels, alphabetical and numerical, as if we were motor-cars; or be known by such figures as are convicts and policemen. And all this would not involve any direct question of misconduct. We might hear Gurgles shrieking across the tennis court, "Play up, K.P. 7983501, old thing; we've got to go on to M.M. 9018972's to tea." Or one of her young friends would be heard saying languidly, "Chuck us a cig., Q.B. 9973588; I've left my filthy case in X.Y. 318220's car." And in all this there could arise no particular criticism of morals, whatever the crabbed and cantankerous might offer in the way of a criticism of manners. There is nothing erotic or even too emotional in those alphabetical forms of address. There is nothing calculated to inflame the passions in the figure 7983501. Our criticism of it would be that it dulled the edge of fine cultural intercourse; that it let us down to a lower level of artistic interest and invention; or, as Gurgles would prefer to say, that it is a bloody bore. It takes away certain fine shades of personal interest, of appropriateness or inappropriateness, which help the coloured comedy of life. For though one Gloria differs from another Gloria in glory and even every Gurgles does not gurgle alike, there is always some artistic interest, serious or humorous, in the association of an individual person with an individual name, perhaps carrying memories of legend or history. But our chief objection would still remain the same; that it is barbaric and reactionary to destroy these cultural distinctions between one thing and another; because it is like rubbing out all the lines of a fine drawing.

Now there were many things in which the Victorians were quite wrong. But in their punctiliousness about etiquette in things like this, they were quite right. In insisting that the young lady should be called at one stage Miss Vavasour, and only at another stage Gloria, and only in extreme and almost desperate cases of confidence Gurgles, they were a thousand times right. They were maintaining a wholly superior social system, by which social actions were significant, and not (as they are now) all of them equally insignificant. There is a meaning in each of those names, as there is a meaning in a name given in baptism or a name given in religion; there is no meaning in the name that is merely a number. When first we are presented to Mr. Robinson, he ought to be presented as Mr. Robinson. The formal title and the family name mean that he is what he is, whatever else he is. He is a man and a free man and a fellow citizen and a person living under the protection of a certain social order. In short, it means that he is worthy of a certain kind of respect and consideration, *before* we know anything else whatever about his worth. If we afterwards reach such a degree of spontaneous friendship as to wish to call him Belisarius, or whatever his first name may happen to be, we shall have done so because we have formed certain independent opinions of our own, about qualities in him which we did not know of at the beginning; and the change will therefore have an intelligent and intelligible meaning. It will be a record of something real in our minds and in his mind. The automatic adoption of his first name by everybody creates an atmosphere of utter unreality. When I was a boy there was a real symbolism, a real poetry, and in the sane sense a real romance, in the transition from being supposed to call a lady Miss Brown to being allowed to call her Mabel. I do not discuss, of course, the dark infernal underworld where she was sometimes called Miss Mabel. The transition did not mean (as the silly sentimentalists who write against the sentimentalism of their grandmothers probably imagine) that you were in love with Mabel; it did not necessarily mean that you were even flirting with Mabel; but it did mean something. It meant that she felt a certain confidence in you and did not object to counting you among her particular personal companions. Today it means nothing at all. And intelligent people have a strong objection to things that mean nothing at all.

There is also this further point. The old stages of intimacy were individual, and in that sense even unconventional. The new comradeship is entirely conventional. It is in the exact and solid sense a convention. The old admission to special friendship occurred at different stages with different people; it was an adventure. The new familiarity is really a formality. It is a thing made common like the rules of a game; it is a thing dictated by what the instinct of the people themselves calls "the crowd." But the essential point about it is that this sort of simplification merely impoverishes life. Life is much more rich and interesting when there are individual initiations, special favours and different titles for different relations of life. This is a real and serious social criticism; and you do not get rid of it by ranting or sentimentalizing; either by saying that Mabel by being called Mabel is well on the road to being called Jezebel; or by saying that in allowing half a hundred men to call her whatever they choose, she is heroically emancipating herself from the tyranny of Man.

I fancy that a real advance in progress and civilization would do exactly the opposite. If I were constructing a Utopia, which God forbid, I should describe a higher civilization in which every human being had a hundred names; in which each had a particular name known only to a particular friend; in which there were more and not less ceremonies differentiating the various kinds of love and friendship and in which the suitor had to go through ten names before he got to Glory. That would be a Utopia really worth constructing; for it would really be a question of construction. Most of the Utopias represent only a dull sort of destruction; the sort of destruction that we call simplification. It would really be something like fun to invent a ritual; but since the neglect of religion, no man has really had the courage to invent a ritual. It would be a great lark to draw up a code of law, decorating Tom, Dick and Harry with their Seven Secret Names. But these things will not come until the modern world has realized that its cure lies in distribution and even in differentiation; and not in mixing up everything together in one great mess. Comradeship has become a sort of Combine; bearing the same relation to true friendship that a Trust does to true trade. Nobody seems to have any notion of improving anything except by pouring it into something else; as if a man were to pour the tea into the coffee or the sherry into the port. The one idea in all human things, from friendship to finance, is to pool everything. It is a very stagnant pool.

I have taken only this one type of a general tendency, because it does not mix the matter up with gushing morality or more gushing immorality. It gives some sort of chance for a little dry light of social criticism. And on a critical consideration, I repeat that these things seem to me a mere decline in civilization; like the beginning of the Dark Ages.

III. ON KEEPING YOUR HAIR ON

IN these essays I appear in the disgusting character of
one advising a pause for thought; advising not only the
young to think what they are doing, but also the old
to think what they are denouncing. And as doing
things and denouncing things are both quite easy, as
compared with thinking about them, we are confronted
from the first with a general and healthy human preference for talking rather than thinking. A special difficulty arises out of the nature of talk, especially modern
English talk. Nothing is more misleading than the
things that are always connected in language, though
they are not connected in logic. There are certain com-
binations of words, with which we are so familiar that
we think they are congruous, when they are really incongruous. We see it most clearly in that excellent and
very English form of humour we call Nonsense. We
instinctively connect the Cat and the Fiddle; though
many of us could distinguish a difference between being soothed at twilight by the melody of violins and
by the melody of cats. Yet the words seem somehow
akin; perhaps there is something in the coincidence
that connects cats and cat-gut. Many Victorians like
myself vaguely feel that a Walrus is the same sort of

animal as a Carpenter; though a logician like Lewis Carroll could duly tell us that they are not only different characters, but different categories. They are not really near enough even to be contradictory, or mutually exclusive. Absolutely in the abstract, I suppose, a walrus might be a carpenter, as a beaver may be a builder; though it may be more difficult to imagine a carpenter (by a mere act of will) becoming a walrus. Yet in that happy borderland of the English fancy, I imagine and I hope that the Walrus and the Carpenter will always walk hand in hand. Hamlet achieved the same sort of wild wedding of words when he said that (given a suitable condition of the wind) he knew a hawk from a hand-saw. And the wise commentator will eagerly note that it was for talking nonsense like this that he was sent to England. For Hamlet was a singularly English sort of Dane; and the wise man truly said, " 'Twill not be noticed in him there; there the men are as mad as he."

No Englishman who loves his country will have any profane wish that his countrymen should leave off talking nonsense. But while they have added a new note to literature in the nonsense of Lear and Lewis Carroll, they may well be warned against too complete and serene a confidence in nonsense, as the only way of settling their social and political problems. And one effect of this exaggeration is that any number of things

are lumped together that do not really or reasonably go
together, any more than cats and fiddles, or hawks and
hand-saws, or the walrus and the practice of carpentry.
These incongruous things are strung together, always
in the form of phrases and often in the form of fashions. They are to be accepted in a lump or rejected
in a lump. The young generally swallow them whole
and the old generally spew them out entire. And the
trouble is that, if you and I attempt to explain that
the things are not at all like each other, and ought not
to be lumped together, we have the appearance of being pedantic—or of being moderate, which is worse.
We seem to be drawing a fine distinction if we venture to doubt, as a matter of practical falconry, that
the hawk and the hand-saw are birds of a feather. We
seem to be debating a fine shade, if we question whether
a fiddle can be used as a mouse-trap or a cat is an orna-
ment to a concert. And even in the world of Wonder-
land, if we say there are some features by which a Carpenter can be distinguished at sight from a Walrus, we
are only asked scornfully what the difference can be
'twixt Tweedledum and Tweedledee.

I will take one small example, which has become a
large and rather sprawling example. It used to be said
that all politics were discussed at the barber's; and in
our time all ethics and philosophy have a tendency to
revolve round the hairdressers. There is a curious tend-

ency to talk about everybody's hair, as the external emblem of everybody's head and heart. The parting of the hair is treated as the parting of the ways; as the mysterious final choice between good and evil; as if the hairdresser was already training the hair into haloes or into horns. The first discussion about modern fashions, and their alleged relation to modern faults, was made to turn almost entirely on a taste in *coiffure*. It is as if the day of judgment were indeed a demonstration that the hairs of our head are all numbered. On some heads there are not so many as there were; and by some fashions it would seem that the task of omniscience was considerably lightened. Some Moslems do indeed believe that the angel will lift them to heaven by the one lock left on a shaven head; and some modes of modernity may yet give a similar meaning to the phrase that Beauty draws us by a single hair. But even the poet who used that phrase might have been surprised at the importance of the hairy test, like that of the hand of Esau. And even a modern man of science might be sceptical about whether the whole problem of human love and hate can be explained by capillary attraction.

Now if I were to take this one case of hair, I should certainly be accused of splitting hairs. I should make certain distinctions which seem very obvious to me, but which would seem very fussy and fastidious compared with the sweeping generalizations on one side and the other. "Let us distinguish," said the envious foreigners; "let us distinguish," are words which may still linger among the last readers of Matthew Arnold; and in this matter I appear in the character of an envious foreigner. When the fashion first came in for women to cut their hair shorter, there were but two loud outcries, triumphant or tragic, from the old-fashioned or the new-fangled. The Victorian veteran would say nothing except: "There they go, bobbing and shingling and breaking down the barriers of right and wrong, blowing the very basis of society to destruction, because they cannot be content to look as beautiful as their grand-mothers." And the new generation, pursuing the new fashion, could apparently say nothing except: "Yes, here we go bobbing and shingling and so by these simple methods bringing in a brighter and broader hope for the future of humanity; since it is only by our own bold effort and adventurous courage that we have avoided being our own grandmothers." Neither of these two outbursts impresses me very much; because one seems to be classing things together merely because they are fashionable, and the other merely because they are not familiar. If I am really to take hair as a social symbol, the first thing that strikes me is that the symbol called Bobbing is very nearly the opposite of the symbol called Shingling. Bobbing means letting the hair flow freely, to about the length to which a great part of humanity, during a great part of history, has thought it convenient to let it flow or fall. Bobbing in itself is a very normal and even traditional thing. It has not been done in many cases by women; but it might have been, without disturbing the general scheme of decoration or dignity. It does not seem incongruous in a picture of Joan of Arc, of which all the rest is in a strictly and even severely mediæval spirit. It is very common in mediæval pictures, especially in those later mediæval pictures which merge with the Renaissance; a great majority of men's portraits show precisely that square-cut cap of hair. Despite the historical legend about short-haired Roundheads and long-haired Cavaliers, the same was really true of the early seventeenth century. Some dandies doubtless wore very long curls and some lunatics cropped their heads to show they were not dandies; but most sensible men of both parties wore something that would now be called a long bob. The great Lord Strafford bobbed his hair. Oliver Cromwell bobbed his hair. In the time of Charles the First all sorts of people wore their hair moderately short. In the time of Charles the Second they began to wear other people's hair immoderately long. But this particular interpretation of moderate length made sufficiently numerous appearances in all periods of history, on Greek vases, in Gothic illuminations, in paint-

ings from Perugino to Van Dyck and from Van Dyck
to Reynolds, to make the general conception familiar
in the case of men and not really startling in the case
of women. But shingling is quite a different sort of
notion. Shingling is shortening and often almost shav-
ing, which would have been thought rather odd in
many other societies besides our own. In any time, it
would have been thought a queer thing for women. In
any time except our time, it would have been thought a
queer thing for men. For it is simply the snobbish
imitation of a particular sort of cheap "hair-cut" which
has become the convention for men (God knows why)
within the last few years. It is the sort of hair-cut that
is meant to go with a billy-cock hat; and we may hope
will go with it—never to return. In its complete and
logical form, when there is really a close shave and a
masculine parting, it is appropriately branded with the
base and snobbish title of an Eton Crop. That name
alone would be enough to show how much there is in
such a movement of liberty or enlargement of the mind.
When ladies go about boasting that they have a Bor-
stal Crop, I will believe in them as real revolutionists.

But the point is that a thing like the Eton Crop
would have seemed eccentric in any civilization, and
according to eternal principles. If a woman had appeared in any antique or mediæval city with half her
head shaved, people would have thought it was some

sort of extraordinary penance. They might have gone on their knees before the saintly humility that could accept such a disfigurement. They might have recoiled in horror, wondering for what nameless sin the wrath of the gods had blasted her with such a sign. I shudder to imagine what they would have thought if the lady had added to the shaven head, as some ladies have been known to do, the ghastly lopsidedness of a single eye-glass. But that horrid emblem does illustrate what is really involved. A single eye-glass is not a question of prejudice or unfamiliarity. It would be equally hideous in the other epochs; it is equally hideous in the other sex. There is not, and never was, any reason in earth or heaven or hell for a woman wearing it, except that some men are silly enough to do so—for a short time, under the terrible patience of heaven. It is against all possible permanent principles of the balance and dignity of the human form. To be monocled is literally to be one-eyed. And the French proverb is indeed true; for if that one-eyed man is king, it must be among the blind.

Now, I have taken that trivial test of the treatment of hair, since it is so frequently made to figure in discussion, as an example of what I mean by discriminating according to permanent principles, instead of blindly accepting or blindly rejecting according to fashion or reaction. It is just possible that, after beginning with the condition of the hair, some daring thinker may go on to consider the condition of the head. He may examine what are called new ideas, and inquire whether they are true ideas; not whether they are as new as they were, in a world where they are bound to grow old. He may ask what Confucius or Aristotle would think about Bolshevism, not merely what Sir William Joynson-Hicks says about Bolshevism; just as I have speculated on what a Greek or a Florentine would think about Bobbing, and not merely what our own aged aunt living in Cheltenham does happen to say about Bobbing. He would inquire whether the progressives themselves know what is the goal of the Path of Progress, not whether their gloomier relatives regard it as the Road to Ruin; just as I would hint (in the delicate matter of hair) that we need some saner principle than a perpetual idea of progression; which must end either with the Bearded Woman or with the Bald Woman.

It is some such desperate task that I shall attempt in the next essay. I shall try to point out that a number of modern notions, about Divorce and Democracy and Free Love and Free Thought and things of various kinds, are in fact notions that have no more to do with each other than the tusks of a walrus have to do with the tools of a carpenter, and less than the long hair of a poet has to do with the short hair of a prize-fighter.

As I have introduced the matter here with the prefatory parable of hair-dressing, I may conclude by noting that this inconsistency in innovation appears the instant we examine any of the innovations in feminine fashion. We all know that there are sombre social critics ready to compare the Modern Girl, at the very mildest, to Jezebel; and we all know that Jezebel painted her face and tired her head and looked out of the window. The critics would willingly credit the modern Jezebel with jumping through the window (indulging in window-crashing as a variation of gate-crashing), and certainly they would assure us that she will imitate the ancient Jezebel by going to the dogs. That the case is rather more complex than that, might be symbolically indicated even in the two acts of adornment. The Victorian Woman tired her head and refused to paint her face; the Modern Woman paints her face, but refuses to tire her head. But I am interested in her head in a different sense; and my real fear is that, in a sense quite different, it does tire her head to think. If I have paused in passing to play with the tangles of Neaera's hair, I think the tangle is inside as well as outside her head.

IV. THE COWARDICE OF COCKTAILS AND OTHER THINGS

MOST of the modernizers are so much concerned to boast that their art is a Jazz pattern that they tend to forget that it is a pattern. Most of its social results are as much cut to a pattern as any Victorian fashion-plate. This is up to a point quite consistent with common sense; but it is not consistent with the extreme claims to liberty and originality that are actually made for it. A dance can be danced to ragtime; but it cannot be wholly and solely a rag. The fullness of freedom could only be found if all the couples were dancing to different tunes. Perhaps it would be even more in the liberal spirit of the age, if even the partners were divided upon the point and the lady danced the Can-Can or the Carmagnole, while the gentleman gravely trotted round the room to the tune of "The Bluebells of Scotland." But the ultimate moral would be the same which a thoughtful mind will discover in so much of current fashions and fictions. On that showing, the perfect relation of the sexes would consist in their not being related at all. So that the last orgy of divorce and independence would end in the separation of monks and nuns. But it would be amusing if they were jumping monks and skipping nuns; if the ballroom were dotted with isolated dancers, each shouting his own accompaniment to guide his own footsteps. Certainly, under these conditions, it would be easier for one individual to go swinging down the room, roaring the air of the Wagnerian Wedding March, while the corresponding bride or bridegroom whirled far away in frantic gyrations to the tune of "I'm off to Callao," or a Czechoslovakian movement expressive of being divorced for the fourth time. Then only could we say that we had Free Dancing, after the manner of Free Verse. Otherwise it is obvious enough that any social action has an element of convention. But these social actions have a very large element of convention. What is called "a daring costume" only means a costume which dares to be a little more conventional than the rest. For in this particular phase of fashion, that sort of daring is itself the convention. If any lady ventured to appear in the conventional costume of exactly twenty-five years ago, she indeed might claim to be unconventional.

Now it may be natural to follow the fashions because, in one sense, it is natural to be artificial. It may be that fashions are the expression of both sides of the human paradox: that desire for a perfect system which creates Utopias, and that failure of every system which creates revolutions. And, in the case of the fashions, we know at least that they have the virtue of vanishing very quickly; whereas, in the case of the Utopias, there is always just the horrid hint of possibility that one of them might remain. But when we make every allowance for fashion as a human habit, we may make two demands of it on behalf of human reason. One is that we should be allowed to call a fashion a fashion, and not be called upon to worship it as an evolution pointing to the end and perfection of man. The other is that we should be allowed to compare one fashion with another, in a calm and level-headed manner, as if we were comparing two Chinese or Egyptian dynasties almost equally remote from us; and that we should not be embroiled in silly political squabbles about progress and reaction when we do so. We are not accused of holding up the whole march of mankind, because we happen to like the Doric column better than the Corinthian column or the pointed Gothic better than the flattened Tudor arch. We can use our common sense about things that are too old to be old-fashioned.

Now I have endeavoured to point out that there are some of these changes of fashion which are changes for the worse, intrinsically and intelligently considered. It is not a question of comparing the new fashion with the old fashion, or the old fashion with the new; but of comparing them both with right reason and all the things that survive every fashion in turn. We are not judging the new convention in the light of the old convention it has destroyed, any more than in the light of the newer convention that will soon destroy it. We are prepared to consider all three as if they existed side by side or had passed through history in the reverse order.

Thus there are some quite recent developments, especially in America, which we may truly call intrinsically idiotic. Their silliness is a thing of simple logic; they would have been made game of by Aristophanes or Erasmus or Voltaire, as much as any Victorian or Post-Victorian could make game of them. The upholders of Prohibition, strangely enough, seem to be quite proud of the fact that many are buying motor-cars instead of wine or beer. For my part, I think it rather more foolish merely to rush from one place to another and back again, and pay money for wind (not to mention dust) than to pay money for wine, with its not quite extinct accompaniment of wit. But at least we may admit that motor-cars were meant to move, and that young people may naturally like them to move fast. But that young people should go and sit in motor-cars that do not move at all, in order that they may drink the wine (or rather spirits) which they are not allowed to drink decently in the dining-room—that is simply a half-witted and humiliating manner of playing the goat, or some much more degraded animal. Its imbecility is in its essence; it has nothing to do with any customs or conventions to which we are or were attached; and no customs or conventions should be able to reconcile us to it. If Aristophanes were called on to consider a hero and heroine who hid in a chariot without any horses, in order to worship Dionysus with such secret rites, he would think the hero and heroine were not very heroic. If Voltaire had put into a satiric romance a lady and gentleman who could only pledge each other when they were inside the coach that was inside the stable, we should recognize that the satiric romance was more satirical than romantic. Yet this custom is now quite common in the great Dry Democracy; and sitting in the motionless motor seems to be regarded by some as quite a wild adventure of youth.

It is sometimes complained that the ultra-modern youth is critical. It does not seem to me that those thus employed shine in the function of criticism; and certainly not of self-criticism. And there are a good many milder forms of folly, even in England, which one would expect to see criticized by a very critical generation. I fear that in most cases these things do not represent any real criticism at all; that whatever element there may be of impudence is not really intellectual independence, but is much more like that very ancient thing that has been complained of in all ages as the "thoughtlessness of youth." Personally, I think it a very agreeable quality. But it is rather too much to ask us to take anything seriously, merely because it takes everything lightly. I may add here, in parenthesis, that of course all this is equally true of the many modern manifestations which are really modern improvements. These also seem to me to be mostly instinctive and artistic, rather than intellectual and philosophical. And these also can only be properly appreciated in relation to the rest of history and the normal standard of humanity. Much of the popularity of sports and games is really classic as well as human; we all know that an ordinary game of tennis can be in the fullest sense a graceful and beautiful thing. But here again we do not test the new life merely by its novelty. An ancient Greek like Aristophanes would instantly appreciate the real beauty of athletics, and of garments or habits suited to athletics. But the ancient Greek would like them because they were ancient quite as much as because they were modern. In fact he would not care about their being either; but only about their being completely human and therefore humane.

But as we are concerned here with criticism, I may return to the case that I have taken for convenience on this occasion; the case of the new customs that have arisen round what is called the Drink Question. Now there is a human and eternal philsophy of the Drink Question; and three-quarters of the present trouble arises from not facing what it really is. It could not be better illustrated than in the way in which people quarrel over what is called the Cocktail Habit. The quarrel is as much a habit as the cocktail; and neither is referred back to any independent reason. Here perhaps the old buffers have a slight advantage over the young boozers; for being drunk is a matter of fact, while being Victorian is only a matter of fashion. But the old buffers do not know how to defend their own fine shade of drunkenness; nor could they give any particular reason for thinking a Dry Martini as deadly as a Martini rifle, while regarding a Benedictine as a Benediction.

Now I have watched the cock-fight about cocktails with all its crowings and scratchings, with some interest; I have heard snobbish praises and priggish reproofs. But I have hardly heard anybody remark on the most interesting thing; the real reason for cocktails. Perhaps it would be fairer to say, one of the two or three real reasons for it. The reason is Prohibition; or the morality that was the making of Prohibition. In other words, the reason was Hypocrisy. It is worth remarking, when the cocktail has become the pledge and symbol of a social life boasting of frankness and freedom. The Bright Young Thing is the better for brazening it out; but she is the worse for having selected, of all things, as a thing to be brandished, a thing that was really invented in order to be concealed.

Cocktails are perhaps the only practical product of Prohibition. They are certainly, I should imagine, the only part of Prohibition in which America will really succeed in setting a Great Example to the world. But the way in which the Prohibitionist morality operated is obvious enough. The reason why the American millionaire does not drink wine or beer with his meals, like all poorer and better Christians, is simple if not dignified. It was summed up admirably by an American in an excellent cartoon in *Life;* a cartoon entitled "Henpecked." He prefers to be a Prohibitionist on public occasions; especially those highly important public occasions when he meets his wife. Hence arose, originally, the habit of the males of the party consuming hurried, secret and very potent drinks before they assembled at the table. It was necessary that the sort of drink should be one that could be gulped down quickly; it was necessary that it should be very strong for its size; and it was natural that it should be made a sort of separate science of luxury in itself. Later, of course, the case was complicated by other modern movements, and some sections of feminine society becoming 'fast society. But that was what determined the novelty and the nature of this remarkable sort of refreshment. It was, quite simply, a tippling husband hiding from a nagging wife. It is not a very noble origin even for a modern mode.

Now this fashion of accepting fashions from anywhere or anybody, and merely as such, has, as in the
present case, produced fashions that are really inferior,
even as such. America happens to be teetotal (in
theory) and America happens to be very rich; and for
these two rather undignified reasons we are bound to
accept the dregs of its secret drinking. We are to swill
the rinsings of its ridiculous cocktail glasses, like sneak-
ish servants or schoolboys after a dinner-party; instead
of drinking decently at our own dinner-table after our
own dinner. These historical origins of the thing explain but do not excuse. The Cocktail Habit is to be
condemned, not because it is American or alcoholic,
not because it is fast or fashionable, but because it is,
on a common-sense consideration, a worse way of
drinking; more hasty, less healthy, even less desirable
to anybody left to the honest expression of his own
desires. It is not Victorian or Edwardian; it is not peculiar to Victoria any more than Vespasian; it is rudimentary human nature that it is more natural to sit still
and talk, and even drink, after dinner, than to stand
up and gulp before dinner.

I know it is possible to hear a feeble voice pleading,
in the defence of these things, that they give a man
an appetite for his meals. Perhaps the last touch is
given to their degradation and destruction, by this be-

ing said in their defence. The cocktail is the coward's drink; in the light of its actual origins in America. The cocktail is the weakling's drink; even in the light of the excuses made for it in England. In the first aspect, it is unworthy of a generation that is always claiming to be candid and courageous. In the second aspect, it is utterly unworthy of a generation that claims to keep itself fit by tennis and golf and all sorts of athletics. What are these athletes worth if, after all their athletics, they cannot scratch up such a thing as a natural appetite? Most of my own work is, I will not venture to say, literary, but at least sedentary. I never do anything except walk about and throw clubs and javelins in the garden. But I never require anything to give me an appetite for a meal. I never yet needed a tot of rum to help me to go over the top and face the mortal perils of luncheon.

Quite rationally considered, there has been a decline and degradation in these things. First came the old drinking days which are always described as much more horrible, and which were obviously much more healthy. In those days men worked or played, hunted or herded or ploughed or fished, or even, in their rude way, wrote or spoke, if only expressing the simple minds of Socrates or Shakespeare, and *then* got reasonably drunk in the evening when their work was done. We find the first step of the degradation, when men do not drink when their work is done, but drink in order to do their work. Workmen used to wait in queues outside the factories of forty years ago, to drink nips of neat whisky to enable them to face life in the progressive and scientific factory. But at least it may be admitted that life in the factory was something that it took some courage to face. These men felt they had to take an anæsthetic before they could face pain. What are we to say of those who have to take an anæsthetic before they can face pleasure? What of those, who when faced with the terrors of mayonnaise, eggs or sardines, can only utter a faint cry for brandy? What of those who have to be drugged, maddened, inspired and intoxicated to the point of partaking of meals, like the Assassins to the point of committing murders? If, as they say, the use of the drug means the increase of the dose, where will it stop, and at what precise point of frenzy and delusion will a healthy grown-up man be ready to rush headlong upon a cutlet or make a dash for death or glory at a ham-sandwich? This is obviously the most abject stage of all; worse than that of the man who drinks for the sake of work, and much worse than that of the man who drinks for the sake of play. And this judgment has nothing to do with prejudice or period or age or youth; but is such as any rational sort of rationalist, however young, ought to be able to see for himself. I am well aware that any number of nice people drink cocktails; that they do not always do it basely and morbidly for this reason; that they often do it more nobly and honourably, for no reason. But that does not make such rationalists very much more rational.

V. GATES AND GATE-CRASHERS

IBSEN, or one of the Ibsen characters most representa-
tive of Ibsen, spoke in a famous phrase of the New
Generation knocking at the door. He did not foresee
that the New Generation would be more likely to
enter without knocking. The character in question was,
of course, the Master-Builder, whose very noble title
came from the craft guilds of a simpler time; and who
ought, by his very title and type of mastery, to have
been specially interested in doors. The door is an excellent concrete symbol of the sort of social limitation
or permission which it is now alleged that the New
Generation tends too much to ignore. And perhaps
Ibsen himself would have understood some problems
more profoundly and sympathetically if he had understood that there is some value even in a real Doll's
House, if it has a real door. The Master-Builder should
understand the mystery of the Door as well as the mystery of the Tower; and none the less, if he has made a
tower too big for himself to climb and a door too small
for himself to enter. Anyhow, the phrase will serve
very well as a sort of summary of the social problem
so often put before us of late; the problem of what is
called the general decline of manners, and especially

of domestic habits that should be dignified by manners.

Dr. Nicholas Murray Butler has lately offered a grave warning about the growth of coarse and careless habits in such things; all that may be symbolized by the New Generation, not so much knocking at the door as banging on the door, barging into the door, breaking down the door, falling through the door, and so on, in an elegant confusion. It so happens that there is a slang name for it, in London at least, which instinctively fastens on this same image of the door and the mode of entry. We call it in modern England Gate-Crashing. It means, as everybody knows, I imagine, the habit of certain hilarious parties of the new youth forcing or insinuating themselves into houses or gardens on festive occasions, where they doubtless display every charm and social qualification, except the slight formality of being acquainted with their host or having been invited by anybody. To dance to a total stranger's Hungarian band; to drink somebody else's champagne without even paying for it, let alone being asked to drink it, is in the mind of these people distinguished in some fine metaphysical manner from ordinary theft and house-breaking. For my part, if I am to make any metaphysical distinction, I very much prefer the house-breaking. To begin with, it is much easier to find arguments for Communism among the poor than for Communism among the rich. And, to go on with, an act of ordinary burglary is at least an example of what, among the rich, is called Private Enterprise. It is more honest than some methods of private enterprise adopted by Big Business; but the essential point is that, because it is not Big Business, it is really private business. Also, it is really an enterprise; in the old chivalric sense of a lonely adventure and a solitary quest. It is at least an example of true Individualism. But the Gate-Crasher is not an individualist, but a Communist. The notable quality of these people, the prevailing character of them and even the most plausible excuse for them, lies in the fact that they have always drifted about in great droves; headless, impersonal crowds, of which half the people did not know what they were doing or where they were going; some of them blind drunk and all of them blind, in the sense of blindly following the leaders who were not there. It is this chaotic communistic character which seems to me to be both the worst evil and the best excuse. It is amusing to note that the very phrase "crowd" has passed from a democratic to an aristocratic sense. Or at least, shall we say, a plutocratic sense. A real rowdy rabid human-hearted crowd of the common people, breaking windows and hanging people on lamp-posts, has become rare and even unknown in England; and is less common than it was even in France, America, Scotland and Ireland. But when Giggles Gunnersbury (the private pet name used by everybody out of every gutter to describe the Duchess of Gunnersbury) enters into a light-headed conspiracy with "Pig" Pomeroy (second son of Lord Portcullis, as of course you know) picking up Vilna Viper, the film-star on the way, and they all drift away to inflict their drunkenness on Mrs. Green, whom they do not know from Mrs. Grundy—when this Arcadian revel occurs, I say, it is quite certain that each one of them will say vaguely that he or she always goes about with "that crowd." So does the great Mob that has at least made history, and achieved the Commune or the Massacre of St. Bartholomew, sink to be a snobbish name for a narrow clique. So does the Boston Tea-Party sink to be the Brighton cocktail party, and the storming of the Bastille end in the storming of the back-garden.

Sometimes there is something more like a conspiracy, or at least something a little more than a crowd. I have known bands of Bright Young Things who really bound themselves together to get past the barriers of some particular party, to which they were not invited, by elaborate strategy of false names or false tickets of invitation. Their lofty minds had lost all prejudice against forgery as well as burglary. A friend of mine, who moves in much more aristocratic circles than I should care to do, invited me to his supper party, warning me that it was necessary to take complicated pre-

caution against sham guests. He therefore provided me
with about five different passes, passwords or proofs
of identity, each more secret and melodramatic than
the last; in the hope that the Gate-Crashers would at
least be unable to reproduce the whole portfolio of
checks and counter-checks, with which the genuine
guest was provided. This all seems to me mere lunacy,
which is the very opposite of liberty. For lunacy by its
nature tends to all these checks, doubts, scruples, se-
crets and inhibitions; it is a net or tangle in which the
mind is caught and loses its freedom. I cannot imagine
any more insane complication, than that of a society
where people engineer laborious and futile frauds,
merely in order to go where they are not wanted; or
where a person has to surround his house with social
man-traps, in order to meet the men he really wants.
On the whole, however, the sort of barging bad manners of which I am speaking is really too barbarous for
such subtlety, and especially for such secrecy. I take
it as the sharpest and clearest case of that coarsening
of manners, of which Dr. Butler writes; because the
whole question of manners, and to some extent of
morals, is bound up in the image, if not of the Gate-
Crashers, at least of the Gate.

Gate-Crashing would be better than it is, if it were
as bad as it sounds. I could feel some sympathy with
it, if it were really the bursting of barriers, by some

bodily dash and daring on some relatively honourable excuse; such as drink or a revolutionary thirst for blood. Here again, as in all these quarrels of the two generations, we must be careful to hold the balance fairly between those generations. Rowdyism and destructiveness are not new; but this is not merely a question of rowdyism and destructiveness. A certain amount of random wrecking and smashing, by excited youth, is not at all peculiar to this generation. The old gentleman ragged at Oxford, though he rebukes the young lady for ragging in Mayfair. But alas, we do not often hear gates actually crashing in Mayfair. If we did, we should feel happier than we do. To hear the huge portals and pillars of the actual mansions of dukes and bankers swaying as in earthquakes or smitten as by thunderbolts, would be bright and cheery in comparison. A noise as of many English butlers hurled down marble steps or shrieking death under falling Adam ceilings, would be fresh and reviving to a democratic heart. I could almost forgive anybody, even ladies and gentlemen, who would bash in the whole frontage of some funereal houses in Belgravia or Berkeley Square. Let none say that here or elsewhere I am without sympathy for the sports of the young, or even of the young of the present generation. There is even now something to be said for them, and there might be something to be said for gate-crashing, if it really were gate-crashing.

But in fact a fundamental and vital truth comes in here; on which hinges the whole question of the dignity and beauty of life, as a Gate swings upon its own hinges. The Gate-Crasher might claim that there is an instantaneous beauty in the Crash; only there is an immortal beauty in the Gate. All culture, all creation, all life worth living, is a thing of Gates.

But the Gate-Crashers do not really go in for gate-crashing. They go in for gate-ignoring; for gate-forgetting; for gatelessness. And that is a very different thing and a very vile and dismal and desolate thing. I mean that they go through life ignoring gates, disregarding doors, not even noticing frontiers or landmarks; and so never realizing that very shape and plan of civilization which gives all its interest to life. It is indeed a curious coincidence that this phrase about the Gate-Crasher should ever have come into use in such a case and in such a condition of society. It was not meant to be mystical, but it is. It may be a coincidence, but it is something like a portent. For the most glorious and significant of all human creations is a Gate. It does not exclude like a wall. But it does not admit as by accident, like a hole in a wall. It is both the assertion of a right and the surrender of a rite. It has a gigantic gesture, in which there is all courtesy, all magnanimity, all hospitality, all humanity: "This is mine . . . but it is yours." It is an invitation by one living thing to another living thing to come into the interior of its life; and there is no dignity in that union unless there is also a wall of separation; unless the two are divided in the sense of independent. The gate is the vision; for it is the point at which alone the one can look into the other. Thousands of painters and poets and ordinary lovers of landscape, must have noticed that intensified impression of a landscape seen under an arch. That is the most vivid instance of the paradox that the part is greater than the whole. It is the only real defence of Property, because it is not only a defence, but a deference; it is the sign of its highest privilege, which is hospitality. In short, the door, the threshold, the limits of the domestic domain, far from being a meaningless thing to be ignored, is a thing far more full of meaning than anything that these people have ever noticed in all their meaningless lives. To say of a thing, "This is where one sort of world ends and another sort of world begins," is to say the magic words which are the essence, not of mere decorum or even of mere dignity, but of all that is really meant by adventure and freedom and romance. That is why the old Pagans, who knew a great deal more than the new Pagans, used the word "Portalis" of temples or typical and emblematic figures, and why Mr. Belloc has used it in the classic manner of his invocation in the sonnet that begins:

What are the names for Beauty? Who shall praise
God's pledge He can fulfil his creatures' eyes?

and then answers his own question in the lines:

But I will call you Beauty in the Gate,
Ambassadorial Beauty, and again
Reconquering Beauty, come to order Fate;
Beauty, salvation of the souls of men.

That is truly and actually the sort of Beauty that is
seen like a vision under the arch of a gateway; the
vision in the gate. It may be a coincidence, but it has
always struck me as symbolic that this precise function is recognized in that passage in the Apocalypse,
about the heavenly city: "He shall call its walls salvation, and its gates praise." Walls do stand for salvation
in the practical sense that people are safe behind a wall.
And gates are really the gap and glimpses that create
praise; the opportunities of beholding from without
the beauty that is within. The city that is without
Gates is without God. Or, if we prefer to put it in the
ancient Pagan fashion, the Gates of the City are the
Gods of the City. Or if we prefer to put it in the vulgar
modern fashion, anybody who really wishes to deliver
the Goods must be like Samson and deliver the Gates.
Now, mad as it may seem, that is the sort of funda-

mental fact of human nature that the new generation
has got to understand, before it understands anything
at all. And I have a certain sympathy with the new
generation, because it is not generally confronted with
this sort of fundamental fact. It is only too often confronted merely with a sort of superficial solemnity.
When the young people disregard doors or other de-
tails of manners, as understood in the immediate past,
they are only told that they have disregarded particular
conventions of the immediate past, or distressed particular people, who rather obviously date from the immediate past. They are not told clearly that the real
meaning of a door is not a convention, and is not a
thing of the past, still less of the immediate past. It is
an eternal dogma about the right relations of human
beings; because human beings, while they cannot live
without some change and some adventure, also cannot
live without some privacy and some protection. And
the door and the dogma will outlast the present drifting fashions, just as they outlived any number of other
fashions that have already drifted away. I have taken
here one working example, the rude invasion of the
privacy and property of others, but the argument applies to a dozen other things, and is the only answer
to this problem about the instability of modern manners. For instance, the young are not told *why* they
should defer to the old, though the ideal is one that is

in the most accurate and appropriate sense, as true as death. It would be impossible to explain why that courtesy is a part of culture, without discussing some of the deepest things in life; including death. They are not discussed, and nothing is said to the young man except, "Your Uncle Hiram was deeply shocked"; or "What your great-aunt Abigail would have thought I cannot imagine." The young man is left under the impression that he is only getting on the wrong side of Uncle Hiram, whereas he is getting on the wrong side of Socrates and Confucius and Dante and Shakespeare and the whole cumulative culture and ordered imagination of mankind. He is simply becoming less like a civilized man; more like a barbarian; more like a baboon. But because he has not yet become quite a baboon, but is still visited by gleams of human reason, you cannot expect him to admit that he is wrong in disregarding the courtesies of the older culture, unless you tell him why. It takes some time to explain, but very few people even try to tell him why. Much of the lapse which Dr. Nicholas Murray Butler lamented is due to a queer sort of vagueness. I have noted already that it is shown even in the language of the time. The young man will say, when feebly following a gate-crashing expedition, "Oh, I'm going with this crowd to that crush." As who should say, "I am vanishing with this vapour into that fog." This undoubtedly makes it more difficult to give the real and rooted reasons for the habits of all human culture. But the young men are not alone to blame; and many of the others are as vague about why they are right as he is about why he is wrong. But in any case, the point is that we must not only tell him sharply to mend his manners, or even to mind his manners. We must tell him to mind his mind.

VI. THE UNPSYCHOLOGICAL AGE

As I began these essays in the hope of irritating everybody by impartiality, which is the most irritating thing I can think of, I propose to conclude them on the same quiet but none the less discordant note. In a recent article, on the one side, I denied that the Victorian Age was the Age of Virtue. I shall here deny that the period of the present generation is in any sense whatever the Age of Pleasure. I think there is a great deal less actual pleasure at this moment than there was in the days of my youth or in most of the days of my ancestors. It is true that a great many worthy moralists denounce the present time because of the prevalence of pleasure-seeking. It may be true, indeed it probably is true, that there is a great deal of pleasure-seeking. But there is a great deal of difference between pleasure-seeking and pleasure-finding. Indeed it might be maintained that the very fury with which people go on seeking pleasure is a proof that they have not found it.

But this generation is full of such depressing paradoxes. The first and most comic is the thing they call Psychology. This generation is everlastingly talking about Psychology. This generation knows nothing whatever about Psychology. It knows far less about

Psychology than any generation of our civilized past; possibly even any of our savage past. It does not know, for instance, the perfectly simple meaning of the Greek word, still less the profound meaning of the Greek myth. I suppose these psychologists have heard of the legend of Cupid and Psyche; but I doubt whether it has ever occurred to them to connect it with their own monstrous Goddess called Psychology. Anyhow, even in that case, it is significant that they would understand the grosser better than the more delicate element in the story. Many of the modern fashion may be said to know, or at least to claim to know, rather more about Cupid than about Psyche.

But the point here is their comic ignorance of the very idea they are always talking about. They even use the word wrong. They talk about it as if it were a particular disease and not a general science. It we read a passionate and heart-searching modern novel (which God forbid) we may open any page and come on a sentence like this: "Maurice fascinated Daphne by his exquisite understanding of her psychology." This is exactly as if I were to say: "I should like to meet Maurice and give him a good hearty kick in the physiology." So indeed I should; but I should not express my just and natural aspiration in such illogical terms. Physiology is not his body, but the study of his body; and Psychology is not his mind, but the study of his mind. Understanding Daphne's Psychology ought not to mean understanding her character, but understanding the books she has written, the lectures she has delivered or the theories she has held on Psychology in general. And if I know anything of Daphne, she has never meddled with such nonsense. Or somebody will say, in a more scholarly work: "The Psychology of Attila, the Hun, has never been scientifically studied." Which is like saying that his Geology has never been adequately studied. The Hun, happy fellow, had no Psychology and no Geology. He could lay waste the earth without asking what it was made of and enjoy himself without asking what he himself was made of. Many human beings, without being Huns, have in the past managed to enjoy themselves a great deal without bothering about Psychology. Still, if a whole human generation is going to bother and bewilder itself with Psychology, it might as well know something about it. The present generation knows nothing about it.

What the present generation knows is a number of catch phrases taken from one particular theory, which happens to be the last theory, and which will therefore be blown to bits by the next theory. But even before it is blown to bits, the culture of our time has never had anything except bits of it. It has learnt for instance, to use the phrase "Inferiority Complex" to describe what Christians used to call Modesty and gentlemen good manners. But if you stop somebody who has just used the phrase "Inferiority Complex," and ask him whether there is such a thing as "Superiority Complex," he will gape and gobble and gurgle unmeaning sounds and his legs will give way beneath him. His inferiority complex, anyhow, will be instantly and appallingly apparent. For he has never thought about the phrase he uses; he has only seen it in the newspapers. The new phrase is not in the newspapers; and he has never heard of it. But the much older and much more profound Psychology of the Christian Religion was founded on the very ancient discovery that a superiority complex was the beginning of all evil. He will also talk to you about the Œdipus Complex; the story of the heathen who murdered his father and did other odd things thought likely to brighten the lives of all "Bright Young Things." But if you ask this great apostle of science to look at the word Science where it is embedded in the word "Conscience," and think about it, you will find that he has never noticed that it is there. These new complexes are not very complex. Compared with the subtlety of the old spiritual ideas, their simplicity is babyish.

But the point here is this; that these young psychologists are backward even as babies. They have not learnt the alphabet. They have not realized even the rudiments of the study of which they talk so much. In every way, of course, we live in a period when people know the last word about everything without knowing the first word about it. They are all like people set to decode a cypher without having ever learnt to read or write. Scores of people will talk to you about the wonderful work of Einstein, not one of whom could tell you what were the primary principles of Newton. An infinite procession of idiots will discuss the Dawes Plan who have never read The Declaration of Independence. But in the case of Psychology, this is particularly true and particularly disastrous. Our fathers did not talk about psychology; they talked about a knowledge of Human Nature. But they had it; and we have not. They knew by instinct all that we ignore by the help of information. For it is exactly the first facts about human nature that are now being ignored by humanity.

For instance, if there is one obvious and outstanding truth of psychology it is what might be called the law of contrast. A lady who wishes to look striking in a black velvet dress does not stand against a black velvet curtain; a man painting a red figure of Mephistopheles does not paint him standing in front of a red-brick villa; and fireworks are not exhibited against a background of fire but against a background of darkness. One would have thought that that principle of the

human mind was plain and obvious enough for anybody to observe it. Yet the whole of modern pleasure-
seeking is missing all that it seeks because nobody will
observe it. If people are to appreciate a pleasure it must
be what children call a treat. It must stand out against
the background of something else that is not quite so
bright as itself. Otherwise we might as well try to
paint in white on a whitewashed wall. I have seen no
sign of this Age of Psychology having appreciated this
elementary psychological fact. Mr. Aldous Huxley remarked, in a brilliant article the other day, that those
who are now pursuing pleasure are not only fleeing
from boredom, but are acutely suffering from it. It is
no longer a question of A Good Time Coming; for
The Good Times have gone with the arrival of A Good
Time All the Time. Mr. Huxley is no romanticist or
sentimentalist, or what some call "Mediævalist"; he is,
if ever there was one, a realist. But he confessed that he
sought out the rude and secluded villages where there
are still what our fathers called Feasts. That is, there
are still festive celebrations of particular dates and events,
which people feel as exceptions and enjoy as exceptions. But men cannot even enjoy riot when the riot is
the rule. The world of which I speak has come, by this
time, to boasting of being lawless; but there is no fun
in it, because lawlessness is the law. I happen to be a
person who has no tendency at all to tedium; I can

truly say that I have hardly ever been bored in my life. I have often amused myself by thinking how amusing it might be to be in a howling wilderness or on a desert island. The only glimpse I ever got in my life of the hell of unbearable monotony, of something I felt I would rather die than endure, was in some of those films describing the fast and fashionable life of New York. Then for one instant I understood what is meant by the agony of being satisfied, or as we used to say, sated.

Another and analogous example is the psychological fact that a man can only concentrate on one thing at a time. He cannot get all that is to be got out of listening to a poem while he is also solving a crossword puzzle. Some will advise him to lay aside the puzzle, others to hurl away the poem; most of us would probably say it depends on whose poem. But anyhow, all of us might be expected to see that fact easily and plainly enough. To judge by the fashionable facts of the hour, none of us can see it at all. Friends ask each other to dinner for a quiet little chat, in restaurants where they have to howl at each other through the noise of a brass band; and cannot utter the lightest jest or the most delicate compliment without making certain that it is louder than the big drum. They will not listen to the music and they cannot listen to the conversation. If these people are pleasure-seekers they are certainly the prize idiots of all human history in their manner of seeking it. For an idiot surely deserves a prize for idiocy when he manages to destroy two pleasures by one action; and kill two singing-birds with one stone.

Now the fashionable world around us is full of such idiocy. It may be said that youth was always thoughtless. The Age of Psychology is the first in which a visitor from outside might suppose it to be brainless. In the old days the village squire went hunting and enjoyed the hunt. He did not have the village organist to carry the church organ behind him on horseback all the way, that the squire might listen to the tune of "Onward Christian Soldiers," at the same time as he was crying "Tally ho!" Common sense, that extinct branch of psychology, told him that he was not likely to enjoy both emotions to the full at the same moment. Hector drove his chariot and enjoyed the chariot-race, and doubtless regarded himself as a very fine fellow and worthy of being commemorated by Homer. But Hector did not expect Homer to run behind his chariot all the time with a large lyre, reciting the "Iliad" lest a single moment of literary appreciation should be lost. Human reason, to which the men of antiquity attached a strange importance, illuminated his mind with two truths; first, that driving horses to win a race is not the best moment for enjoying a recitation; and second, that the poet running behind might be rather

too much out of breath to recite well. But inconsisten-
cies and inconveniences quite as ludicrous as that throng
around us in the contemporary hustle and hunt for
pleasure. I conclude, therefore, that whatever else the
hustlers know about, it is not the thing that they talk
about; and that their chief mark is a quite unprece-
dented ignorance of psychology.

There are a great many other ways of stating the
weakness; there are a great many other and more serious problems in which it is displayed. I had thought
of concluding on some of these graver cases of confusion and lack of logic; on the chaos and contradition
that marriage and divorce and free love have made between them; on the perpetual chatter about private
enterprise side by side with the ever increasing disap-
pearance of private property and private independence;
upon the bottomless and bewildering nonsense of the
new suggestions for a faith without a creed. But all
these are only graver manifestations of the weakness
of the man who goes to a noisy tavern for a quiet dinner, or takes a friend to whom he cannot talk to a
concert to which he cannot listen.

VII. THE TRUE VICTORIAN HYPOCRISY

THE most essential educational product is Imagination. It is a wandering and even wild Imagination that all schools should chiefly instruct all school-children. For Imagination will teach them how to live a quiet and humdrum life.

This simple truth is now much neglected both by the fashionable and the old-fashioned. The way to make people contented is to make them creative, not to make them barren. I have no desire to lock people up in the parlour or the pantry, or deny them excursions and excitements. But it is strictly true that the larger is their Imagination, the less they will mind being locked up in the parlour; or, for that matter, in the coal-cellar. The child who can see the pictures in the fire will need less to see the pictures on the film. The man who can make up stories about the next-door neighbour will be the less dependent upon the next day's newspaper. So long as the minds of the poor were perpetually stirred and enlivened by ghost-stories, fairy-stories and legends of wild and wonderful things, they remained comparatively contented; possibly too contented, but still contented. The moment modern science and instruction stopped all these things, we had a Labour Question and the huge discontent of to-day. Both for good and evil, but especially for good, it is Imagination that keeps people quiet.

On the other hand, dull people always want excitement. Three-quarters of the real luxury or prodigality or profligacy, that is complained of just now, is due to the dullness of people who cannot imagine anything they do not experience. They are so miserably and dismally stupid that they actually have to do things. They are so poor in spirit that they have to have things. They have to have a flying-machine fitted up with every luxury, because they cannot send their souls up while flying a kite. They have to be in a racing car in order to believe that it really races. If this principle of the inner life were understood, we might today restore the sanity of civilization; and especially the poetry of the home.

I have already explained the object of these essays: it is to suggest a criticism of the new generation, that shall not merely suggest a complacency about my own generation. I am not a venerable Victorian objecting to plus-fours because they are different from peg-top trousers; but rather because they are not different enough. I should not complain of Oxford bags because they would have caused a mild surprise to Tom Brown at Oxford; but because they would have caused a mild surprise to almost anybody else. Alexander about to conquer the world, Alfred called upon to reconquer the Wessex kingdom, would certainly have received them with the fervent expression; "Not in these trousers." But it is less true of trifles than of serious truths. And this distinction especially applies to the blunders made by both generations about the fundamental human institution called the Family or the Household.

Half the trouble has arisen from two falsehoods; both of them current, not so much among those who are young enough to be troublesome, as among those who are old enough to know better. But in both generations there is a fixed idea; first, that what is called the Victorian Age was a golden age of domestic respectability and unity; and second, that there was something specially British about this solid and conventional family life. The very name of Queen Victoria is supposed in some way to stamp a sacred domesticity upon the period and the place, and to suggest that the idea of the family was at its highest or strongest in that age and in that country.

Both these ideas are quite false. The Victorian age was not one in which domesticity was at its highest. On the contrary, it was one at which domesticity was at its lowest. Half the present evil arises from the fact that the Victorians never did understand the virtues that they were vaguely supposed to defend. It is as if we were to say that the Catholic religion and the

French monarchy were at their healthiest and most hopeful moment in the time of Voltaire. In the eighteenth century there were still bishops for Voltaire to make fun of, as in the nineteenth century there were still British matrons for Bernard Shaw to make fun of. But the matron no more embodied all that was meant by the Mother or the Madonna than an Abbé who was a sycophant was like an Abbot who was a saint. Mrs. Grundy was not really a good wife. We know it—because we never hear of Mr. Grundy. The Age of Mrs. Caudle's Curtain Lectures was not a noble summit of the noble sacrament of matrimony, towering over such monuments of marriage as the Taj Mahal and Charing Cross.

Now the Victorians were people who had *lost* the sense of the sacredness of the home. They still believed in the respectability of the home; but that is only another way of saying that they wanted to be respected by other people for reverencing what they did not really reverence. If we compare Victorian customs with the customs of the mass of mankind, the first thing that will strike us is that the purely domestic customs have been cut down to next to nothing; that they are duller and not brighter, colder and not more convivial. It is as if we were to say that because a Victorian banker generally disapproved of walking about naked, therefore his age was the golden age of glorious and flamboyant costume. The truth is that he had cut down costume to something meaner and more prosaic and less significant and important· than costume had ever been before. He wore chimney-pot hats and mutton-chop whiskers because he thought less and not more about the possibilities of dress than did a gallant of Giorgione or a cavalier of Van Dyck. He preferred the chimney-pot hats as he preferred the chimney-pots to the Tower of Giotto. He tolerated the mutton-chop whiskers as he tolerated the mutton-chops; because he despised French cookery along with French culture. It is quite possible for a sympathetic imagination to see something manly and bracing about such a Philistine. But nobody, however sympathetic, would say that he understood the real meaning and possibilities of dress. Nor did he understand the meaning and possibilities of domesticity.

To begin at the beginning, we can invoke not merely the Christian but the Pagan idea of the family. The Pagans actually had Household Gods. They worshipped the house; they treated it as a temple; not metaphorically but literally. They sacrificed to gods who were conceived as present in that place, as distinct from other places. The gods presided over the most material and even grotesque features of domestic life. Now the more modern man of the Manchester School did not go on like that. He did it less than any

other man of any other school. He was never tempted
to bow down in worship to the door-scraper. He was
never known to offer sacrifices to the umbrella-stand.
But in the old heathen culture, the door-scraper would
really have been an idol or the umbrella-stand a god.
The umbrella-stand would at least have been dedicated
to some deity who might be supposed to be interested
in umbrellas; presumably Jupiter Pluvius. The door-
scraper would have stood for a ceremony; and the
ceremony of scraping the feet would have been one of
purification or lustration; of discarding the dust and
mire of the world. So far from the Victorian heavy
father having these traditional feelings, he had them
far less than the majority of mankind. The satirists who
poked fun at him talked about his furniture as his
household gods. But the satirists who poked fun at him
paid him far too fine a compliment. He did not see
any special significance, artistic or religious, in the Victorian furniture around him. He did not have mahogany tables because his dreams brooded on the dark
red forests filled with the mysterious red men of the
West. He did not have black horse-hair sofas because
there rushed through his imagination a gallop of wild
black horses. He did not even have cut-glass chande-
liers to express his lofty meditations on the mystery of
the Prism, which shatters the daylight into colours and
stains the white radiance of eternity. Any inquiry ad-

dressed to a prosperous banker about the year 1855, upon these points, would substantiate my statement. The banker was not thinking poetically about his furniture; and he was not really thinking mystically about his home. He wrote letters to *The Times,* or read letters in *The Times,* in which was conventionally used the phrase, "The sanctity of the home." But he never really meant sanctity; he only meant security. I mean that he had not the idea of sacredness as compared with his own Christian forefathers, or his own Pagan forefathers or even his own Pagan contemporaries. When he went to China (which he did occasionally, in search of money) he saw a Pagan civilization very like the old Greek and Roman civilization. There also the house was a temple. There the religion of the family flowered or flamed into all sorts of fantastic expressions which the British merchant thought very ridiculous. Coloured lanterns glowed on days of domestic festivity and gorgeous paper dragons were waved like banners. But the Victorian did not want to wave any dragon. The Victorian was never known to dance about with a coloured lantern. The notion of the *poetry* of private life had faded from him and his generation, and seemed to be something not merely alien but barbarous. In order to understand what can be made of the religion of the family, he would have

-᪽68᪽-

had to learn from a yellow Chinaman; the last thing he would be likely to do. True; he had something at home called Family Prayers; and the mere memory of them has murdered religion for two generations.

This was the real Victorian hypocrisy; at least, this was the real falsity of the Victorian claim. They did to some extent pose to their children and grandchildren as the traditionalists. But they had in fact been the great anti-traditionalists; and it was their time that destroyed a thousand traditions. They did sometimes quote Horace or Virgil about hearth and altar; but there was never any flame upon their altar, even if there were a dying fire upon their hearth. They did sometimes talk about household gods, as if their houses had been full of holy images. But in truth it was they and not their children, who were the iconoclasts. Nineteenth-century England had destroyed the last legends of the fireside, long before twentieth-century England had a chance of feeling the full poetry of the legend. The Philistines were the image breakers; they shattered the household gods and the patron saints. Puritanism combined with Industrialism threw away the Lares and Penates like the disused dolls of a dead infancy and went on to what was counted the manhood of the Manchester School; with what results we see today. And so completely did they dry up that fountain of fairy-tales which flows from China to Peru, that I shall now probably be charged with uttering a "paradox," because I say something so self-evident as that it is the homestead and the inner chamber, the dwelling-place of Imagination.

The generation in revolt fled from a cold hearth and a godless shrine. That is the historical fact that is really hidden by both sides in this controversy. It is supposed that they revolted against what their elders called religion and they called superstition; against what their elders called domesticity and they called drudgery. But those elders were not really religious; they were not even really domestic. This was notably the case in the English middle class, which puffed itself out with preposterous spiritual pride about its domesticity. It actually had the impudence to talk about French immorality; when the French sense of the family was twenty times stronger than the English. The English had their own special merits of sport and adventure; but they were definitely undomestic as compared with nearly everybody else. They exiled all their children to boarding-school; and thought any boy a milksop who admitted any affection for his mother. The chief reason for regarding a Frenchman as a fool (a thing essential to the national self-respect) was that he confessed to a certain respect for his mother. It was from *this* sort of chilly and half-inhabited house that the rebels escaped to conduct their revels in hotels and night-clubs. In my next essay I shall take them in their turn; and affectionately explain to them what fools they are, for doing anything of the sort.

VIII. MARRIAGE AND THE MODERN MIND

I HAVE been requested to write something about Marriage and the Modern Mind. It would perhaps be more appropriate to write about Marriage and the Modern Absence of Mind. In much of their current conduct, those who call themselves "modern" seem to have abandoned the use of reason; they have sunk back into their own subconsciousness, perhaps under the influence of the psychology now most fashionable in the drawing-room; and it is an understatement to say that they act more automatically than the animals. Wives and husbands seem to leave home more in the manner of somnambulists.

If anybody thinks I exaggerate the mindlessness of modern comment on this matter, I am content to refer him to the inscription under a large photograph of a languishing lady, in the newspaper now before me. It states that the lady has covered herself with glory as the inventor of "Companionate Divorce." It goes on to state, in her own words, that she will marry her husband again if he asks her again; and that she has been living with him ever since she was divorced from him. If mortal muddle-headedness can go deeper than that, in this vale of tears, I should like to see it. The newspaper picture and paragraph I can actually see; and stupidity so stupendous as that has never been known in human history before. The first thing to say about marriage and the modern mind, therefore, is that it is natural enough that people with no mind should want to have no marriage.

But there is another simple yet curious illustration of modern stupidity in the matter. And that is that, while I have known thousands of people arguing about marriage, sometimes furiously against it, sometimes rather feebly in favour of it, I have never known any one of the disputants begin by asking what marriage is. They nibble at it with negative criticism; they chip pieces off it and exhibit them as specimens, called "hard cases"; they treat every example of the rule as an exception to the rule; but they never look at the rule. They never ask, even in the name of history or human curiosity, what the thing is, or why it is, or why the overwhelming mass of mankind believes that it must be. Let us begin with the alphabet, as one does with infants.

Marriage, humanly considered, rests upon a fact of human nature, which we may call a fact of natural history. All the higher animals require much longer parental protection than do the lower; the baby elephant is a baby much longer than the baby jellyfish. But even beyond this natural tutelage, man needs something quite unique in nature. Man alone needs education. I know that animals train their young in particular tricks; as cats teach kittens to catch mice. But this is a very limited and rudimentary education. It is what the hustling millionaires call Business Education; that is, it is not education at all. Even at that, I doubt whether any pupil presenting himself for Matriculation or entrance into Standard VI, would now be accepted if flaunting the stubborn boast of a capacity to catch mice. Education is a complex and many-sided culture to meet a complex and many-sided world; and the animals, especially the lower animals, do not require it. It is said that the herring lays thousands of eggs in a day. But, though evidently untouched by the stunt of Birth-Control, in other ways the herring is highly modern. The mother herring has no need to remember her own children, and certainly therefore, no need to remember her own mate. But then the duties of a young herring, just entering upon life, are very simple and largely instinctive; they come, like a modern religion, from within. A herring does not have to be taught to take a bath; for he never takes anything else. He does not have to be trained to take off a hat to a lady herring, for he never puts on a hat, or any other Puritanical disguise to hamper the Greek grace of his movements. Consequently his father and mother have no common task or responsibility; and they can safely model their union upon the boldest and most advanced of the new novels and plays. Doubtless the female herring does say to the male herring, "True marriage must be free from the dogmas of priests; it must be a thing of one exquisite moment." Doubtless the male herring does say to the female herring, "When Love has died in the heart, Marriage is a mockery in the home."

This philosophy, common among the lower forms of life, is obviously of no use among the higher. This way of talking, however suitable for herrings, or even for rats and rabbits, who are said to be so prolific, does not meet the case of the creature endowed with reason. The young of the human species, if they are to reach the full possibilities of the human culture, so various, so laborious, so elaborate, must be under the protection of responsible persons through very long periods of mental and moral growth. I know there are some who grow merely impatient and irrational at this point; and say they could do just as well without education. But they lie; for they could not even express that opinion, if they had not laboriously learnt one particular language in which to talk nonsense. The moment we have realized this, we understand why the relations of the sexes normally remain static; and in most cases, permanent. For though, taking this argument alone, there would be a case for the father and mother parting when the children were mature, the number of people who at the age of fifty really wish to bolt with the typist or be abducted by the chauffeur is less than is now frequently supposed.

Well, even if the family held together as long as that, it would be better than nothing; but in fact even such belated divorce is based on bad psychology. All the modern licence is based on bad psychology; because it is based on the latest psychology. And that is like knowing the last proposition in Euclid without knowing the first. It is the first elements of psychology that the people called "modern" do not know. One of the things they cannot comprehend is the thing called "atmosphere"; as they show by shrieking with derision when anybody demands "a religious atmosphere" in the schools. The atmosphere of something safe and settled can only exist where people see it in the future as well as in the past. Children know exactly what is meant by having really come home; and the happier of them keep something of the feeling as they grow up. But they cannot keep the feeling for ten minutes, if there is an assumption that Papa is only waiting for Tommy's twenty-first birthday to carry the typist off to Trouville; or that the chauffeur actually has the car at the door, that Mrs. Brown may go off the moment Miss Brown has "come out."

That is, in practical experience, the basic idea of

marriage; that the founding of a family must be on a firm foundation; that the rearing of the immature must be protected by something patient and enduring. It is the common conclusion of all mankind; and all common sense is on its side. A small minority of what may be called the idle Intelligentsia, have, just recently and in our corner of the world, criticized this idea of Marriage in the name of what they call the Modern Mind. The first obvious or apparent question is how they deal with the practical problem of children. The first apparent answer is that they do not deal with it at all.

At best, they propose to get rid of babies, or the problem of babies, in one of three typically modern ways. One is to say that there shall be no babies. This suggestion may be addressed to the individual; but it is addressed to every individual. Another is that the father should instantly send the babies, especially if they are boys, to a distant and inaccessible school, with bounds like a prison, that the babies may become men, in a manner that is considered impossible in the society of their own father. But this is rapidly ceasing to be a Modern method; and even the Moderns have found that it is rather behind the times. The third way, which is unimpeachably Modern, is to imitate Rousseau, who left his baby on the door-step of the Foundling Hospital. It is true that, among the Moderns, it is generally nothing so human or traditional as the Foundling Hospital. The baby is to be left on the door-step of the State Department for Education and Universal Social Adjustment. In short, these people mean, with various degrees of vagueness, that the place of the Family can now be taken by the State.

The difficulty of the first method, and so far, of the second and third, is that they may be carried out. The suggestion is made to everybody in the hope that it will not be accepted by everybody; it is offered to all in the hope that it may not be accepted by all. If *nobody* has any children, everybody can still be satisfied by Birth-Control methods and justified by Birth-Control arguments. Even the reformers do not want this; but they cannot offer any objection to any individual—or every individual. In somewhat the same way, Rousseau may act as an individual and not as a social philosopher; but he could not prevent all the other individuals acting as individuals. And if all the babies born in the world were left on the door-step of the Foundling Hospital, the Hospital, and the door-step, would have to be considerably enlarged. Now something like this is what has really happened, in the vague and drifting centralization of our time. The Hospital has been enlarged into the School and then into the State; not the guardian of some abnormal children, but the guardian of all normal children. Modern mothers and fathers, of the emancipated sort, could not do their quick-change acts of bewildering divorce and scattered polygamy, if they did not believe in a big benevolent Grandmother, who could ultimately take over ten million children by very grandmotherly legislation.

This modern notion about the State is a delusion. It is not founded on the history of real States, but entirely on reading about unreal or ideal States, like the Utopias of Mr. Wells. The real State, though a necessary human combination, always has been and always will be, far too large, loose, clumsy, indirect and even insecure, to be the "home" of the human young who are to be trained in the human tradition. If mankind had not been organized into families, it would never have had the organic power to be organized into commonwealths. Human culture is handed down in the customs of countless households; it is the only way in which human culture can remain human. The households are right to confess a common loyalty or federation under some king or republic. But the king cannot be the nurse in every nursery; or even the government become the governess in every schoolroom. Look at the real story of States, modern as well as ancient, and you will see a dissolving view of distant and uncontrollable things, making up most of the politics of the earth. Take the most populous centre. China is now called a Republic. In consequence it is ruled by five contending armies and is much less settled than when it was an Empire. What has preserved China has been its domestic religion. South America, like all Latin lands, is full of domestic graces and gaieties; but it is governed by a series of revolutions. We ourselves may be governed by a Dictator; or by a General Strike; or by a banker living in New York. Government grows more elusive every day. But the traditions of humanity support humanity; and the central one is this tradition of Marriage. And the essential of it is that a free man and a free woman choose to found on earth the only voluntary state; the only state which creates and which loves its citizens. So long as these real responsible beings stand together, they can survive all the vast changes, deadlocks and disappointments which make up mere political history. But if they fail each other, it is as certain as death that "the State" will fail them.

PART II
NEWER YORK

I. THE AMERICAN IDEAL

THERE is nothing the matter with Americans except their ideals. The real American is all right; it is the ideal American who is all wrong. It is the code and conception of life imposed from above, much more than the merely human faults and weaknesses working up from below.

In so far as the citizens of the Western democracy have really gone wrong, they have not inherently or quite naturally gone wrong. They have been taught wrong; instructed wrong; educated wrong; exalted and uplifted wrong. A huge heresy, rather peculiar to modern times, yet singularly uncriticized by modern critics, has actually perverted them in a way which is not really very consonant to their personalities. The real, natural Americans are candid, generous, capable of a beautiful wonder and gratitude; enthusiastic about things external to themselves; easily contented and not particularly conceited. They have been deliberately and dogmatically taught to be conceited. They have been systematically educated in a theory of enthusiasm, which degrades it into mere egotism. The American has received as a sort of religion the notion that blowing his own trumpet is as important as the trump of doom.

It is, I am almost certain, in the main an example of the hardening effect of a heresy, and even of a hostile heresy. There are more examples of it than those admit who ignore the peril of heresy. The Scots are an example; they were never naturally Calvinists; and when they break free, it is to become very romantic figures like Stevenson or Cunninghame Graham. The Americans were never naturally boomsters or business bullies. They would have been much happier and more themselves as a race of simple and warm-hearted country people eager for country sports or gazing at the wonders in country fairs. An egotistic heresy, produced by the modern heathenry, has taught them against all their Christian instincts that boasting is better than courtesy and pride better than humility.

It is queer to note how raw and recent is the heresy; and how little it has been spotted by any heresy-hunt. We have heard much of modern polygamy or promiscuity reversing the Christian idea of purity. We have heard something, and we ought to hear more, of modern capitalism and commercialism reversing the Christian idea of charity to the poor. But we have not heard much about Advertisement, with its push, publicity and self-assertion, reversing the idea of Christian humility. Yet we can at once test the ethics of publicity by removing it from public life; by merely applying it to private life. What should we think, in a private party, if an old gentleman had written on his shirtfront in large fine flowing hand: "I am the only well-bred person in this company." What should we think of any person of taste and humour who went about wearing a placard inscribed "Please note quiet charm of my personality." What should we say if people gravely engraved on their visiting card the claim to be the handsomest or the wittiest or the most subtly, strangely attractive people about town. We should not only think, with great accuracy, that they were behaving like asses, and certainly destroying beforehand any social advantages they might really have. We should also think they were wantonly reversing and destroying a principle of social amenity and moral delicacy, recognized in all civilized states and ages, but especially emphasized in the ethics of Christianity. Yet modern business, especially in America, does really enforce this sort of publicity in public life; and has begun to press it even in private life. But the point to be emphasized here is that it is really pressed upon most of the Americans; they are goaded and driven into this sort of public life; large numbers of them would have been perfectly contented with private life. They would have endured it, even if it had retained all the old decency and dignity of private life. For this is where the critic must deal most delicately with the subtlety of their simplicity.

-⟨85⟩-

The Americans are always excused as a new nation; though it is no longer exactly a new excuse. But in truth these terms are very misleading; and in some ways they have rather the atmosphere of an old nation. Over whole tracts of that vast country, they are certainly what we should call an old-fashioned nation. In no nation in the world are so many people attached to a certain sort of old texts, familiar quotations, or the pieces of sentiment that were written on the pink pages of Victorian albums. A popular book was published, while I was in America, bearing the somewhat alarming name of *Heart Throbs,* from which compilation one might learn that some great and grim judge of the High Court had for his favourite poem "Grandmother's Blessing," or that some colossus of commerce, a Steel-King or an Oil-King, preferred the simple lines entitled, "Daddy's Hat." It is only fair to say that some of these hard-headed and ruthless rulers had never forgotten the real classical claims of "Love's Young Dream," or "The Seven Ages of Man." Some may sneer at these extracts, but surely not at their novelty or crudity. I do not mention them for the purpose of sneering at them, but, on the contrary, for the purpose of showing that there must be a great block of solid and normal sentiment, even of traditional sentiment. And people having that sentiment, people inheriting that tradition, would not necessarily, on their

own account, have become believers in selfish, sensa-
tional self-advertisement. I suspect, as a matter of fact,
that there is rather less of such callous and contemptu-
ous egoism in America than anywhere else. The older
civilizations, some of which I will venture to call the
more civilized civilizations, have a great many advantages in variety of culture and a conspectus of criticism;
but I should guess that their wickedness is more wicked.
A Frenchman can be much more cynical and sceptical
than an American; a German much more morbid and
perverted than an American; an Englishman much
more frozen and sophisticated with pride. What has
happened to America is that a number of people who
were meant to be heroic and fighting farmers, at once
peasants and pioneers, have been swept by the pesti-
lence of a particular fad or false doctrine; the ideal
which has and deserves the detestable title of Making
Good. The very words are a hypocrisy, that would have
been utterly unintelligible to any man of any other age
or creed; as meaningless to a Greek sophist as to a
Buddhist monk. For they manage, by one mean twist
of words, to combine the notion of making money with
the entirely opposite notion of being good. But the
abnormality of this notion can best be seen, as I have
said, in its heathen and barbaric appeal to a brazen
self-praise. Selling the goods meant incidentally, of
course, lying about the goods; but it was almost worse

that it meant bragging about the goods.

There is a very real sense in which certain crudities in the Americans are not so much a part of American crudity as actually a part of American culture. They are not mere outbreaks of human nature; they are something systematically impressed upon human nature. It is not for nothing that some of the most prominent features of their actual academic training are things like schools of commerce or schools of journalism. There is a vital distinction between these things and all that the world has generally meant by a school; especially the most scholastic sort of school. Even those who think little of learning Greek and Latin will agree that it carried with it a vague suggestion of admiring Greeks and Latins. The schoolboy was supposed in some sense to feel inferior. But even in a commercial academy the boy is not occupied in gazing at some great millionaire doing a straddle in wheat, with the feelings of the simplest pagan of antiquity gazing at the Colossus of Rhodes. It would not do him much good if he did; but in general practice he does not. If he learns anything, he learns to do a straddle in wheat himself, or to hope that he will do it as acrobatically as any other acrobat. He does not even learn to venerate Mr. Rockefeller, but only to imitate Mr. Rockefeller.

Nor does the practical study of journalism lead to

any particular veneration for literature. The qualities inculcated and encouraged are the same as those which commerce inculcates and encourages. I say it with no particular hostility or bitterness, but it is a fact that the school of commerce or the school of journalism might almost as well be called a school of impudence or a school of swagger or a school of grab and greed.

But the point is that people are taught to be impudent or greedy, not that they are naturally impudent and greedy. As a matter of fact, they are not. And that is the whole paradox of the position, which I have already suggested and should like here to expand. I have seen in the United States young people, coming out of this course of culture, who actually pulled themselves together to be rude, as normal young people have always pulled themselves together to be polite. They were shy in fact and shameless on principle. They would ask rude questions, but they were as timid about asking a rude question as an ordinary youth about paying a compliment. They would use the most brazen methods to induce somebody to see them, and anybody who did see them would pity them for their bashfulness. They were always storming the stage in a state of stage fright.

The very simple explanation of this puzzling contradiction is that they were perfectly nice and normal people in themselves, but they had never been left to themselves by those who were always telling them to assert themselves. They had been bounced into bouncing and bullied into being bullies. And the explanation is the existence of this modern heresy, or false ideal, that has been preached to everybody by every organ of publicity and plutocracy: the theory that self-praise is the only real recommendation.

I have suggested that the American character might have developed in an infinitely more healthy and human fashion if it had not been for this heresy. Of course the American character would in any case have been very much more alert and lively and impetuous than the English character. But that has nothing to do with the particular features and fashions of commercial advertisement and ambition. There are many other races that are more vivacious or vehement than the English and who yet live the normal life of contented country folk, and practice the traditional ideas of modesty and courtesy.

The trouble with the false commercial ideal is that it has made these men struggle against modesty as if it were morbidity; and actually try to coarsen their natural courtesy, as other men stifle a natural crudity. I do not think that bragging and go-getting are American faults. I hate them as American virtues; I think the quarrel is not so much with the men as with the gods: the false gods they have been taught to worship and still only worship with half their hearts. And these gods of the heathen are stone and brass, but especially brass; and there is an eternal struggle in that half-hearted idolatry; for often, while the gods are of brass, the hearts are of gold.

II. A PLEA FOR PROHIBITION

AFTER a careful study of the operations of Prohibition in America, I have come to the conclusion that one of the best things that the Government could do would be to prohibit everything.

That the story of Mephistopheles, the fiend who tempted Faust, is in reality an allegory of the story of Prohibition in America, is admitted by all serious scholars whose authority carries weight in the modern world. Critics admiring the sarcasm of Mephistopheles have repeatedly referred to his humour as "dry"—a term now impossible to separate from its political content. The promise of the devil to produce a new and youthful Faust, in place of the old one, is obviously an allusion to the promise of the Prohibitionists to produce a new and fresh generation of American youth, unspoiled by the taste of alcohol. The allegory is not only clear about the sort of things that Prohibition promised, but is especially clear about the sort of things that Prohibition really performed. One of the things, for instance, which Mephistopheles really performed (if I remember rightly) was to make holes in a tavern table and draw out of the dead timber some magic hell-brew of his own, saying something like,

Wine is sap and grapes are wood;
This wooden board yields wine as good.

Could there possibly be a more self-evident and convincing reference to the abuse arising from wood alcohol? Any critic who would evade so crushing a conclusion, as if it were a coincidence, must be indeed lacking in the logic that has lent stability and consistency to the Higher Criticism. When the fiend describes himself as "the spirit who denies," it is plain enough that we are to read it in the sense of one who denies people the use of spirits. But the conclusive argument to my mind, in the light of all the circumstances both in literature and life, is the fact that Mephistopheles distinctly says of himself, "I am he who always wills the bad and always works the good."

That Prohibition and Prohibitionists willed the bad no righteous or Christian person will doubt for a moment. That Prohibition and Prohibitionists eventually work the good may appear for the moment more doubtful. And yet there is one sense in which Prohibition has already worked some good; and may yet work very much more good. Wood alcohol is not in itself a happy example; and no judicious wine-taster will expect to find the best vintages in a liquid drawn by a devil out of a dinner-table. But there really is already in America a large number of people who are producing drinks in an equally domestic fashion; and drinks for their own dinner-tables if not out of them. It is not by any means true that all this home-made drink is poison. The presence of the devil is plain enough in the pleasing scheme of the American Government to poison all the alcohol under its control, so that anybody drinking it may be duly murdered; but murder has become almost the ordinary official method of the enforcement of a teetotal taste in beverages.

But the private brews differ very widely; multitudes are quite harmless and some are quite excellent. I know an American university where practically every one of the professors brews his own beer; some of them experimenting in two or three different kinds. But what is especially delightful is this: that with this widespread revival of the old human habit of home-brewing, much of that old human atmosphere that went with it has really reappeared. The professor of the higher metaphysics will be proud of his strong ale; the professor of the lower mathematics (otherwise known as high finance) will allege something more subtle in his milder ale; the professor of moral theology (whose ale I am sure is the strongest of all) will offer to drink all the other dons under the table without any ill effect on the health. Prohibition has to that extent actually worked the good, in spite of so malignantly and murderously willing the evil. And the good is this: the restoration of legitimate praise and pride for the creative crafts of the home.

This being the case, it seems that some of our more ardent supporters might well favour a strong, simple and sweeping policy. Let Congress or Parliament pass a law not only prohibiting fermented liquor, but practically prohibiting everything else. Let the Government forbid bread, beef, boots, hats and coats; let there be a law against anybody indulging in chalk, cheese, leather, linen, tools, toys, tales, pictures or newspapers. Then, it would seem by serious sociological analogy, all human families will begin vigorously to produce all these things for themselves; and the youth of the world will really return.

III. WHICH IS THE GOVERNMENT?

When we say that this is the age of the machine, that our present peace, progress and universal happiness are due to our all being servants of the machine, we sometimes tend to overlook the quiet and even bashful presence of the machine gun. But the machine gun has been overcoming its shyness of late, and has been persuaded to figure in a field where it was never seen before.

In one sense, of course, the machine gun is, like many modern things, so familiar as to be almost old-fashioned. Governments have long used it, of course, against barbarians so brutal and ignorant as not instantly to surrender their own mines or oil fields to the foreign millionaires who govern most of the governments. So an early poem of Mr. Belloc summed up for ever the moral qualities that make for world mastery and the really essential virtues of a conquering race:

> *Whatever happens we have got*
> *The Maxim gun and they have not.*

But an entirely new development has appeared in America, and especially in Chicago. It consists of the organized use of machine guns by the ordinary criminal classes: Bill Sikes, the coarse and common burglar of our boyhood dreams, is no longer defending himself with a pistol, or with a park of artillery.

I do not mean to be at all Pharisaic about Chicago. It has many beauties, including the fine fastidiousness and good taste to assassinate nobody except assassins. Criminal society in Chicago seems to be extraordinarily exclusive; and it is impossible for any mere journalist or traveller to penetrate into the best circles or receive an invitation or "be taken for a ride" (a hospitable formula for death) by the true leaders of fashion. While I was in Chicago a very distinguished individual had the misfortune to be murdered, being caught between the fire of two machine guns and falling with a ton of lead in him. But as I gather that the same gentleman had himself murdered no less than thirty-four persons in exactly the same way, it was impossible to feel that any advantage had been taken of his innocence and youth, or that he had been lured into a game of which the rules had not been explained to him.

It is not every town in the world that has this strict segregation and close corporation of crime. Rather as the art-for-art's-sake school used to maintain that only artists should criticize artists, so these refined gunmen feel that only murderers are competent to condemn murderers. I wish there were a similar rule, in other towns, by which only cheats should be cheated, only swindlers should be swindled, and only usurers should be ruined and sold up, as there is in this elegant conception that only killers should be killed.

Unfortunately, it is by no means true of all the present killing in America. And the killers who take a wider range, the murderers who murder on a larger and more liberal plan, are chiefly the Federal officers pretending to enforce the Prohibition Law. These, as universal patriots, responsible only to the Republic as a whole, have been known to murder quite mild and inoffensive bystanders, on the bare possibility that they are as likely as not to have given or taken a drink. There are some who admire this statesmanlike breadth of action more than the narrow trade union spirit of the fighting boot-leggers of Chicago.

But there has been a new violation of this virginal isolation of the artists in crime; a new method called racketeering. It seems, for some mysterious reason, to be applied especially to Beauty Parlours, which are now very nearly the national industry of America. A gentle-manly stranger enters the shop and asks the shopkeeper whether he wishes his business to succeed. The shop-keeper replies that such was indeed his purpose para-doxical as it may seem, in opening the shop. The stranger then says, "You will leave so many thousand dollars on the counter this afternoon," and disappears. If the shop-keeper neglects this advice his shop is blown up. It seems simple. I cannot quite understand why it is not done everywhere. But anyhow, it is another step outside the self-contained society of mutual murder, and as such regrettable. A member of the F.F.C.K., or First Families of Chicago Killers, should not stoop to associate with people who run beauty parlours. As a mere matter of romance and sentiment, I should be relieved if most of the beauty parlours were blown up; but I draw the line when there are people inside them. Perhaps people are blown up in the very act of being beautified. It would lend a new and impressive meaning to face-lifting.

But this is a parenthesis. What I wish to note as significant and ominous about the murderer and his machine gun is this. It is a commonplace that each of us, coming into the world, sees as a tableau what is in fact a drama. He sees the procession standing still; or it moves so slowly that he can hardly believe it has been moving. The young cannot imagine a world without motors; I can remember it, but I cannot imagine a world without railways. Yet I have met old men who could remember a world without railways. Similarly, I have met very old men who could remember a world without policemen.

That universal and equal pressure of police organization everywhere; the loneliest village policeman in instant touch with Scotland Yard—all that is a comparatively recent thing. It is not so long ago that Bow Street runners in top-hats ran in vain after successful highway-men on horseback; and so back to times when bands of robbers could hold some natural stronghold like that of the Doones or the Macgregors. At other times a robber baron would hold the king's castle against the king; and command companies of bows and spears equipped like the royal army. In other words, the criminal classes were often armed and organized like the police.

Perhaps, after all, it has been but a moment of time in which we have seen poor Bill Sikes reduced to a shabby bludgeon, or a pistol he had to hide in his pocket. Perhaps it is only for a flash that we behold the Victorian vision of the omnipotent policeman. In the advanced, inventive, scientifically equipped and eminently post-Victorian city of Chicago the criminal class is quite as advanced, inventive and scientifically equipped as the government, if not more so. If our modern society is breaking up, may it not break up into big organizations having all the armament and apparatus of independent nations; so that it would be no longer possible to say which was originally the lawful government and which the criminal revolt? God knows there are criminals enough in both of them.

That is the significance of the criminal with the machine gun. He has already become a statesman; and can deal not in murder but in massacre.

IV. A MONSTER: THE POLITICAL DRY

THERE have been any number of speculations about whether America will ever reverse Prohibition. The answer to the question is that America has already reversed it. America, as represented by Americans, has long ago repealed the Volstead Act and the Eighteenth Amendment. America, as misrepresented by American politicians, may take longer to deal with the business, and delay it with endless lobbyings and more or less corrupt compromises; but that is the way of politicians all over the world. In the same sense in which a man might once have said, with some general justification, that America was going dry, it can now be said definitely and decisively that America has gone wet.

I have paid two visits to America, one recently and one about twelve years ago. The change is striking, and even startling, and could hardly be stated too strongly. Perhaps the best way of stating it is this: that in the old days even the Wets were Dry, and today even the Drys are Wet. I mean that, immediately after Prohibition was established, many were hopeful about it who were not Puritans or anything resembling what we understand by teetotallers. Many regarded the Saloon as the source of all sort of social evils besides drink; many rather reluctantly abolished the drink in order to abolish the others. The honest men among them definitely gave up drink for the good of their country. Practical politicians among them, on the other hand, forbade drink to their country and went on cheerfully drinking themselves. These are the only sort that now remain, and even they are tending more and more to an open avowal of their contempt for Prohibition. They are described, with considerable restraint, as Political Drys; instead of being described as greasy humbugs and dirty cowards, as they would be among truthful people. But the remarkable fact is that not only are there now any number of Political Drys, but there is a larger and larger number of Political Wets. As the dishonest Puritans denounce drinking in public and themselves drink in private, so the honest Puritans more and more denounce Prohibition for the public and continue to abstain in private. The decent drinkers were almost in favour of Prohibition, because of the good it might do. The decent abstainers are now entirely against Prohibition, because of the evil it has done.

For all that the social reformer once said against Saloons, he can now say against Prohibition; and he says it. It was once argued that the harm done by the Saloon went far beyond drunkenness. It is now certain that the harm done by the Volstead Act goes far beyond the denial of drink. It was once alleged that the Bar was working with an organization of vice. It is now certain that the Federal Law works by an organization of crime. Perfectly innocent private citizens, men who not only had no liquor on their persons, but had never used it in their lives, have been murdered by gunmen in the name of the Government of the United States. People have been shot at sight, not only without trial, but practically without suspicion and without reason. Men have tried to make Drink illegal; and have only succeeded in making Murder legal. They have not only given an almost complete immunity to professional murderers, so long as they are also bootleggers; they have given a special and peculiar licence for murdering to those whose official duty it is to prevent murder. It is not surprising that even teetotallers begin to feel doubtful about incessantly pouring out blood to prevent somebody else from pouring out beer, and even then not preventing it.

The Political Wet, who is an honest man, is a new figure in politics, and a curious contrast to the Political Dry, who is a hypocrite and a swindler. The latter drinks and forbids drinking; the former abstains, but refuses any longer to enforce abstinence. I have been told by any number of decent American citizens that it will be absolutely necessary to alter the Act, even though they themselves may see no reason to alter their own abstinent habits in this respect. A jolly Irish car-driver said to me. "I tuk Father Mathew's Pledge when I was a boy in

Ireland, and I never touch a drop; but, gosh! I'll never vote for that law again." Indeed, the horror generally felt for some of the results of Prohibition is very largely simply a horror at the effects of drink. One American magazine had an excellent article, which summed up the whole position in the title: "Prohibition is Too Wet." The author explained that he did not mind a reasonable amount of drunkenness and alcoholic disease, but such delirious drunkenness, such blind, blatant, precocious, and ignorant intoxication as had been produced by the Eighteenth Amendment was really too disgusting for any decent person to tolerate.

There are, of course, many fanatical enthusiasts for Prohibition still, but they are the least respected sort of fanatics. This is none the less true because many of them, I am sorry to say, are the ministers of various Christian bodies of the sort which we should call in England Nonconformist. But nobody could form any notion of them by studying English Nonconformists. With many worthy exceptions, they are men who use only the tricks of trade to vulgarize a tradition that is dead, and might at least be allowed to be dignified. It is not a pleasant sight to see people trying to revive the sectarianism of the seventeenth century by the sensationalism of the twentieth. A very refined and scholarly person, himself temperate to the point of ascetism, said to me that certain of the Gospel ministers booming Prohibition were "the

lowest form of animal life in America." And, though
their organization is enormously rich, powerful and dicta-
torial, and though their influence at the time of the first
Prohibitionist hopes was very considerable, I very gravely
doubt whether they are very influential now. Certainly
they are not influential with the influential; least of all
with the intelligent. What will be the effect of the present
condition of negative disappointment and disgust it is,
of course, very difficult to say. But it will be next door
to impossible to work another big rally in favour of
Prohibition.

Public men are, of necessity, uncommunicative. We
might say that public men are, of necessity, private.
The one person from whom it will be most difficult to
extract a real announcement of national policy will be
the man who is set up specially to announce it. In that
respect, Mr. Hoover is neither better nor worse than all
modern statesmen, who are apparently obliged to state
ambiguously what everybody else is stating plainly. But
it is very generally said in America that his ambiguous
statements point to an intention to modify the law rather
than to defend it. He is naturally somewhat hampered
by the fact that his followers got him elected largely
by denouncing Mr. Smith as a drunken blackguard,
merely because Mr. Smith was then saying what Mr.
Hoover would probably now prefer to say. Anyhow,
there is so much unrest on the subject that I doubt

whether the law can much longer remain as it is.

There are rumours which, even if they are only rumours, testify to the unrest. It is said that brewers have already had the tip to begin putting in their plant in certain towns of the Middle West. It is eagerly pointed out that the President did not even say, as commonly quoted, "Prohibition is a noble experiment," but only "Prohibition was an experiment noble in motive," as if expressly reserving judgment on the nobility of its effect, or even its intrinsic idea. It is possible, though improbable, that the President thinks the country may remain dry during his Presidency, and says, less metaphorically, than the old despot, "After me, the Deluge."

Perhaps the strangest symptom of a strange situation is something almost horrible in the *humour* of that situation. Of course, no serious person could ever have taken Prohibition seriously. But the only really serious part of it is that it prevents people from taking anything else seriously. Something that is supposed to be grotesque (God knows why) about the subject of beer has spread a froth of frivolity over all sorts of topics, like the froth overflowing from all the tankards in a pot-house. Facts in the social situation that would have been normally regarded as a subject for horror are now almost inevitably regarded as a subject for humour. There has been a sort of smooth and slippery descent to a lower level of seriousness; a universal bathos and even baseness; a descent like a butter-slide, which might be described as a beer-slide. Naturally it was always a joke that Prohibition was merely a joke; it has now ceased to be even a practical joke. But it is no joke that murder is merely a joke. If murder had been presented to the mind in any other connexion except this comic collapse of idiotic legislation, nobody would have thought it was merely a joke. Yet it is almost unavoidable, through a mere association of ideas, that we should all of us think of the wild antics of civil war between the bootleggers of Chicago as if it were something so ridiculous as to be unreal. When one of the principal bootleggers, caught between the machine guns of rival bootleggers, actually fell to the ground filled with lead, it was apparently impossible not to associate it vaguely with old dead jokes about the drunkard tumbling down when he was filled with liquor. A sort of lurid levity lights up the whole pandemonium like a pantomime. So, in the old pantomimes, I saw a policeman cut up into sausages. But that policeman was not *really* cut up.

This utterly unnatural inversion is a psychological fact, and is not the least of the facts that combine to tell against Prohibition in the minds of really serious men. The very fact that Al Capone has become a sort of burlesque brigand, who might appear in a masquerade, illustrates the loss of something that has hitherto been a true psychological deterrent of crime. He is really and truly part of a masquerade, for he is safe behind a mask, because it is a comic mask. The scar of Scar-Face actually has a disarming effect, like the red nose of the old music-hall comedian. The red nose is not the only shade of red that can come to be regarded as comic. This rather terrible laughter, this universal levity and laxity about anti-social actions, once criticized only seriously, is one of the most disquieting effects of the great disaster of Prohibition. That is why it is now being regretted and even denounced by the sort of people who were once prepared to consider it favourably; nay, who were themselves so serious as to be able for a month or two to take it seriously. They think, with very great justice, that if it goes on much longer nothing whatever will be taken seriously.

Burlesque and parody are almost impossible in our time, because nothing that happens in fancy can be more fantastic than what happens in fact. We have had no good comic operas of late, because the real world has been more comic than any possible opera. Here is a good example in connexion with this particular matter. Lawyers and law-abiding citizens have been gravely debating, in the United States, whether the chief organizer of murder in America may not perhaps be brought to trial for an error in his income-tax return. This is a solid, solemn, and rather awful fact. But I challenge anybody to say whether it would not have seemed quite

quaintly Gilbertian in a Gilbert and Sullivan opera. It
is all the more Gilbertian because it really raises one of
those fine legal or logical quibbles on which so many of
the Savoy operas were made to turn; such as the plea
that the apprentice of the Pirates of Penzance, being
born in Leap Year, could not come of age till he was
four times the age of twenty-one; or the plea that, as the
Mikado's orders must always be carried out, it was right
to report them so, even if they had not been carried out.
There is obviously a delicate and disputable matter of
doubt and judgment as to whether a gentleman can be
made to pay income tax at all upon the profits of a
brewery that is not supposed to exist. The American
President, like the Mikado, declares that a thing cannot
be done, and therefore it cannot be done; and certainly
nobody can be taxed for doing what cannot be done.
All this in its very essence, is like an English comic
opera; but it is becoming even cruder, till it looks like an
American comic strip. It is asking too much of mankind to expect them not to feel it as comic, and the
Americans do feel it as very vividly comic; and yet there
is present all the time the equally vivid sense that it is,
in fact, very tragic. Nay, they feel of such blind blunder
and butchery the worst thing that human things can
feel; that it is too inhuman to be tragic.

I do not think that Prohibition can possibly survive
this crushing combination of humour and horror. That

is why, as I have said, it has now many new critics, among precisely that sort of serious people who have no artistic pleasure in horror, and are even accused by their enemies of having a defective sense of humour. To such people it is bad enough that legislation should end merely in crime. It is intolerable that crime should end merely in comedy. And there is added to all the rest the crowning and capering comedy that the criminals are among the few people who are still in favour of legislation against the crime. It would seem an extraordinary thing to say of any community that nearly all the citizens were Communists, and nobody approved of private property except the burglars. It is really true to say, of many parts of the American community, that most of the citizens are drinkers, and that nobody approves of Prohibition except the bootleggers. By the time that the immoralists are in favour of the veto, the moralists may well be against it. And, to a considerable extent, certainly to a much greater extent than before, they are against it. More and more, as time goes on, the serious social idealists will be against Prohibition. In a sense, we may say that the Puritans are against Prohibition. In a sense, we may yet say that the Prohibitionists are against Prohibition.

Meanwhile, I hope that no one in England or in Europe will make it a mere taunt against the great American democracy that they so swiftly made and unmade this colossal blunder. I think it very possible that more conservative countries, if they did make it, would never recover anything like the spirit to unmake it. It has needed not a little courage and candour and humour to keep up the criticism that has now proved fatal to it, at any rate as a serious social ideal; and I am not quite certain that every country in the world would have been lively enough to have kept that protest alive. There still remain considerable disputes and difficulties about how Prohibition, as a law, is to be abolished. As a fact, it is abolished already. But if it was a rasher people than ours that accepted, it was a bolder than ours that defied it.

V. BERNARD SHAW AND AMERICA

WHEREVER I wandered in the United States people leapt out upon me from holes and hedges with the question pointed like a pistol, with all the promptitude of a gun in the hand of a gunman: "How is Bernard Shaw?" It is not surprising that they should be interested in Bernard Shaw; so are we all, however much we disagree with him, interested in that now thoroughly enthroned and authoritative Grand Old Man; and there is some truth in his own theory that the Americans are especially interested in him because he abuses Americans and will not come to America. It is not surprising, I say, that they should be intensely interested in Bernard Shaw; what is extraordinary is that they should be so intensely interested in me in connexion with Bernard Shaw. They seem to suppose that I am his brother or his keeper; though I admit that, if we travelled together, there might be a dispute among the schools as to which was the keeper and which the lunatic. Sometimes I am almost tempted to think that Shaw and I are the only Britishers they have heard of; or perhaps because one of us is thin and the other fat we figure as buffoons in an eternal dust and dance, like Dan Leno and Herbert Campbell. By this time I am driven to go about declaring that I am Bernard Shaw; the difference is a mere matter of two disguises: of alternative cushions and a beard. And that as I point out, is the real reason why Bernard Shaw cannot come to America.

Well, I hope the association of ideas may be connected with the cordial admiration and affection I have always felt for the most genial and generous of Puritans. But, with all that admiration, I cannot deny that in considering America, and comparing it with Shaw, I have sometimes had darker thoughts. I think, I might say I fear, that Mr. Shaw's refusal to come to America is a bad thing for America but rather a good thing for Mr. Shaw. With a sort of filial piety I would keep from him, if I could, the awful truth of how large a part of America shares some of his Shavian notions; and how very common, not to say vulgar, those notions are when seen on so large a scale. The very things which in aristocratic England seem like the rather distinguished oddities of a sage have, in democratic America, become the dull prejudices of a society. Total abstinence in a man like Shaw is an almost elegant eccentricity; but there is nothing elegant about Prohibition, and it is not an eccentricity but a convention. Shaw would find thousands of Americans to take quite seriously his prejudice against tea or tobacco; but their seriousness would only serve to make him absurd.

In that sense, we may even say that Shaw does well

to keep out of America; because he is the only American in England. The great Fabian faddist would be horrified if he knew how much of America follows his fads; for these things when they begin really to exist, are not fads but fanaticism. Sometimes I think that if Mr. Shaw did come to America he would take to drink, or rather he would take to drinking; a totally different thing. He would walk down Main Street puffing smoke from an enormous pipe which would not, perhaps, prove to be altogether the pipe of peace. For those old nineteenth-century negations of his, those mere distinctions of disgust, would not long retain their dignity in a world where their ubiquity makes them themselves disgusting.

Mr. Shaw, in his amusing confession concerning his habit of abusing America, says with great pride that he has always denounced America as a civilization of villages or a nation of villagers. I am astounded not at the disrespect to America but at the disrespect to villages. I can imagine no more splendid or soaring compliment to any society of sinful men than to say that it is a civilization of villages. I only feel that it is a much more splendid and soaring compliment than modern America deserves. But in so far as it does deserve it, it is in that fact that it retains some of the democratic tradition, or, as some would say, some of the democratic dream. It is true that a peculiar Puritan type of religion has come to stiffen the village life of America, but it is equally true and very important to notice that this Puritan religion did not originally come from the village life of England, still less from the village life of Europe. Puritanism was originally a thing of the towns, especially of the rich merchants and the first modern capitalists. In fact, the Puritan chapels were distributed then just as the petrol pumps are distributed now. That is, they became numerous, but they never became natural. They never, in the true historic sense, became normal. Puritanism always stood toward paganism or papistry as a petrol pump stands to a tree; it may have a reason, but it has not a root; nor can it grow anywhere of itself.

Anyhow, in spite of this artificial admixture in the ancient agricultural life of mankind, the modern agricultural life of America is still the only real life there is. It is, especially, all that remains of the real popular life. Exactly in so far as men are villagers, men are democrats; in so far as they still live in villages, they are citizens: citizenship has vanished from the cities.

Here indeed appears the whole fallacy of Business Training. The weakness of what is called "useful education" is that it does not propose to teach these villagers something that will widen them, but something that will keep them narrow, or even make them more narrow. It will replace Niagara with a petrol pump; a trickle of oil for a torrent of water. Utilitarianism will limit and localize, exactly as Puritanism did limit and localize,

the natural universality of the village. So long as the
village is merely the ancient human village, it is dealing
with elemental and universal things; with water and
fire and the watching of stars and winds, the bearing of
children, the mourning for the dead, the whole naked
and abstract grandeur of the death and life of men. But
so soon as it becomes a modern industrial city, still more
a modern technical school, it shrinks and dwindles to
little and local things; things peculiar to a particular and
already passing epoch; the particular mechanical toys
of our time; the particular medical antidotes to our
diseases. And the proof of all this is in the practical fact,
which almost all intelligent Americans are already beginning to lament.

It can be stated in half a hundred different ways, but
perhaps the simplest way of stating it is to say that a
perfectly vigorous and intelligent young American,
equipped with all the latest devices of mechanics and
chemistry, bursting with all the latest business tips about
salesmanship and mass psychology, is not an educated
man. He is not educated because he has only been educated in all modern things, and not even in all mortal,
let alone all immortal, things. In a word, he has not been
made acquainted with human things, and that is what
we mean when we say that he has neglected the hu-
manities.

Thus Mr. Bernard Shaw's charge of mere rustic

and rudimentary ignorance does not really hit the weak
point of America; though it may in a sense hit the weak
point of Mr. Bernard Shaw. Now I come to think of it,
it is odd that a Vegetarian, who lives on the fruits of the
earth, should be so much cut off from the earth. It is
curious that a man who must often consume the same
sort of roots and salads as a peasant, should be so ignorant
of a peasantry. True, I do not quite know what food Mr.
Bernard Shaw ought to eat, unless it be salt and star-dust
and pure oxygen. But anyhow, in regarding America
as merely rustic, he does not so much condemn it un-
fairly as compliment it too much. In so far as America
retains certain rural truths and traditions, it is exactly by
those, as I shall point out later, that she may yet survive and succeed. But the obvious and outstanding
American feature is that even the ruralism is not rural.
Something may be due to the omnipresence of machinery; much to the omnipresence of newspapers with
their note of town life; more to the habit of treating a
farm not as a farm to feed people, but as a shop from
which to sell food. But anyhow the stranger misses what
is meant in Europe by the rural note. Men are not talking about Land, as they are talking from Siberia to Con-
naught about Land; they are talking about Real Estate.
I know it is often insisted that the celebrated Main Street
was only a village; that is exactly what I mean by my
much criticized remark that America does not contain a

village. In that sense, Main Street is as urban as Wall Street. The tone of discussion, the type of success that is discussed, even the type and look and dress of the men who join in the discussion, strike a European as belonging entirely to the town. I have read in American comic fiction of the Hick and the Hayseed; but I have never seen them in America. Therefore, in the two essays which follow, I must be excused if I use the name of Main Street to express the main bulk of American popular life. I must be pardoned if I am quite sure that Main Street is a Street: much more certain than I am that Gopher Prairie is a Prairie. I may be wrong; but I am not quite so wrong as Mr. Shaw, when he makes the two monstrous suggestions; first, that America is a world of villages; and second, that it would be any the worse if it were.

VI. THE CASE AGAINST MAIN STREET

THERE is one aspect of the great American quarrel between Puritans and Pagans, with the Humanists and the Catholics intervening, in which I have a pretty complete sympathy with Mr. Sinclair Lewis and the attack on Main Street. Mr. Lewis seems to have lived for a long time on the shady side of Main Street; and most streets have a shady and a sunny side. I myself have only lived for a short time on what seemed to me the sunnier side of Main Street; and I was pretty contented with such a place in the sun. But there is a shady side; there is even a dark side. And upon one point the criticism advanced by this famous critic is a fair one.

It was stated to me with great spirit and sincerity by a young journalist from Wisconsin, who told me that he agreed with Sinclair Lewis because the old generation in the Middle West had despised him for liking music and poetry, and considered such things effeminate and even cowardly. Now, in that attitude there really is, or was, a most dangerous delusion, which greatly concerns the fashions and false values of our time. There certainly does or did exist a dim idea, in the minds of many Americans, that a business man is in a special sense a man. It is what is really implied in praising him as a

Regular Guy, or a Red-Blooded He-Man, or a hundred per cent. American. Because he has been dealing with materialistic things, there clings to him a faint suggestion of that very different thing: a mastery of materials.

Man subduing matter is rightly regarded as man asserting himself as man. But man dealing in modern commerce is not man subduing matter. He is, on the contrary, a man more analogous to a mathematician or an astronomer, in that he is dealing with things generally abstract and almost invariably remote. If the enterprising huckster who has just sold a hundred shares in rubber were one who had just been hacking his way through a rubber forest, we might excuse, though we might not admire, his masculine swagger at the expense of an intellectual Jew merely playing on a Jew's harp. But even playing on a Jew's harp might be regarded as an athletic and even an acrobatic feat, compared with merely mentioning in Wall Street that a transaction was to be recorded at a certain figure. If a big business man having a big jeweller's shop on Fifth Avenue could be supposed to have dived for all the pearls in the Pacific Ocean, or even climbed the mountains to find rubies and emeralds in their caverns, he might call himself a He-Man and be pardoned for his simplicity in regarding a violinist as less conspicuously He. But a violinist is much more like a smith or a swordsman or a strong manual craftsman than is a man who merely dresses up in shiny clothes and a smile, and buys and sells pearls that other men have dived for and rubies that other men have dug from the mine. This illusion of a sort of strength or sanity in modern business operations is in fact the chief falsity which poisons our present society.

It was all implied, and summed up, in the remark of a typical plutocratic politician, when he called it Normalcy. That famous phrase did contain the whole false suggestion: that the present buying and selling is normal, as the primitive hunting and fishing were normal. As a matter of fact, they are far less normal than modern fiddling or fretwork. The arts are nearer to the crafts, and the crafts are nearer to the soil, than any of them are to the ghastly abstractions and wild unrealities of speculation and finance. In so far as this was an attitude encouraged among Regular Guys, the Guys were really as irregular as a Guy on Guy Fawkes day in England; they were like a Guy made of paper, or stuffed with straw, or wearing merely a mask for a face. In so far as this was the charge brought by men like Mr. Sinclair Lewis against the Regular Guys, the charge was justified. It was not wholly justified; because there were and are other manlier elements in Main Street; and especially a tradition, not altogether dead, of the pioneering and the personal adventures of the days of Huckleberry Finn. But I cannot insist too strongly on this point,

for it is the whole point of my political thesis: that the
current commercial mode of life is not common human
welfare, or even common human warfare. It is a process
at best indirect and at worst crooked; often a nightmare and always a dream.

Some Englishmen, I believe, have always been in
favour of what they called an Anglo-American alliance.
All Englishmen, I hope, have always been in favour of
an Anglo-American friendship. Above all, all Englishmen, I most ardently hope, will always be opposed to
that most dangerous and degrading of all relations: an
alliance without a friendship. Personally, and for reasons
related to much deeper matters of national and international dignity, I should be very well contented with a
friendship without an alliance. But it is another matter,
for any one who understands either national or international things, to make sure that a friendship is really
friendly. And in this matter as in many similar matters,
there is a bad principle which often expresses itself in
even worse practice.

Some people seem to believe that it is possible for any
person to steer his way through this world, in perfect
sympathy and safety, so long as he selects occasions for
praise and not occasions for blame. Unfortunately, the
principle of praise, in preference to blame, very often
works out like this. The foreign critic, being forbidden
to blame anybody, really decides not to criticize or even

consider anybody. And then the foreign critic, being forced to praise somebody, judiciously decides to praise himself. This is sometimes called Optimism, and is supposed to be a very cheering sight. In plain fact, the critic gives far more offence by praising himself than by abusing all the aliens in the world. Of this kind, for instance, are the Englishmen who praise everything by calling it English. Such a one is certain that any foreigner will dance with delight on being told that his house or church is really quite English; though he ought to know with exactly what amount of delight he would himself be dancing if he were told that Westminster Abbey is quite Turkish or that Shakespeare's cottage is entirely Prussian.

Another way of falling into the same folly is to declare that the Englishman has all good things, and therefore has goodwill; even goodwill to Americans. Many a worthy sympathizer has supposed that he was praising foreigners when he was obviously only praising English charity to foreigners. Doubtless there are plenty of foreign diplomatists who make the same blunder in the process of praising England; but it is a blunder to be avoided by anybody who is praising anything. It would be almost better to impute ill to our neighbours than always to impute good to our neighbours with an air of imputing good nature to ourselves.

But there is one form of this fallacy which is really a

practical obstacle to international sympathy. It is even a practical obstacle to international criticism. It is essentially this: that a man will actually be unable to criticize a foreign nation, because he is unwilling to criticize his own nation, in so far as it is subject to the same criticism. If he began by frankly confessing that his own country had to some extent made the same mistake, he could probably go ahead and really and conclusively prove that the foreigner was mistaken. As it is, he will sometimes be forced cravenly to admit that the foreigner is right, because he is afraid to admit that he himself has ever been wrong.

There are several very practical examples of this very practical problem. For instance, an Englishman, as a European, has a right to complain of the bumptious and purse-proud swagger of some Yankee globe-trotters in Europe. Only he ought to preface his protest by admitting that the same sort of complaint was made about Englishmen in Europe in the days when England had the same mercantile supremacy and the same materialistic mood. After he has said that, he can say anything; he can pursue the vulgar and offensive American with fire and sword of satire and derision and denunciation, and probably find most sensible and responsible Americans agreeing with him. What irritates the normal or rational American is not that he should think Americans blamable, but that he should think himself blameless. I believe this to be a very vital principle of the peace and friendship of nations.

It is therefore essential that Englishmen should be very careful to admit that the real American evil is not so much the result of America breaking away from England as of its having remained only too English. This is so in part, in the *fanciful* nature of finance and commerce. The American tradesman is every bit as romantic as an Englishman. He is in some aspects more than enough of a realist; and yet it is the nature of contemporary commerce that this sort of unreality is a part of reality. We, who propose a return to simpler social relations are always described as reomantics and visionaries and idealists of the impossible. But the truth is that we are the only realists, and the adherents of Big Business are by their very nature unrealists. They have to be unrealists, because so many of their dealings are in unreal wealth or unreal wares. It is of the very nature of finance and speculation to be perpetually taking money out of Lunar Green-Cheeses and putting them into Sunbeam Cucumbers; gambling in Moonshine Consolidated and Mares'-Nests, Ltd.; making profits on merely getting, and then getting rid of, various projects for obtaining figs from thistles and blood from stones. This unreality, in the sense of the remoteness of the ultimate material test, marks a mass of ordinary quite respectable stockbroking; quite apart from any that can be considered in any way disreputable. It is not merely a question of those who start baseless companies, but of those who profit by them in passing without ever knowing for certain if they are baseless or not; without ever dreaming of dealing with the realities they are supposed to represent. But even over and above this question of the unreality of speculation, there is an interesting question involved in the other unreality which is called Optimism. The truth is that the commercialists have to be optimists, —because they live in a world that can so easily go wrong. The business men live in a world of notions; they live in a world of fictions; they live in a world of dreams.

There is a proverb to the effect that farmers always grumble; and it is true that peasants often strike a superficial observer as pessimists. People living close to the land, especially their own land, have a way of talking candidly and caustically about their experiences of life, which does seem almost sulky compared to the sentimental self-encouragement we are used to in journalism and professional politics. It is only when the peasant is known a little better, that it becomes apparent that his free cursing and criticizing of conditions covers a real love of the permanent facts behind them; a solid tenderness for his own soil, a talkative pride in his own knowledge of the tricks of weather or animal life; in short, that sense of being quite at home which is the

origin of his grumbling as well as of his contentment.
But the vital point is that he is a realist, dealing with
realities, and therefore certain that they will remain the
same whatever he says about them. He does not think
that a cloud will come across the sun because he curses
the unsufficiency of sunlight; he does not think he will
bring on a thunderstorm by being in a bad temper; he
does not imagine that he can change the wind with a
word, or dry up the dew by confessing to a fit of depression. But the business man does believe these things,
and in his own mad business world he is right. He knows
he *can* cloud the fortunes of some speculation, by speaking against it, or bring on a crisis by permitting a criticism; or ruin a prosperous season with a whisper, or
create a depression merely by being depressed. Therefore he has to be an Optimist, poor devil; poor, dear,
dreary, miserable devil.

Moses in *The Vicar of Wakefield* has become the
type of all that is unbusiness-like, because he bought a
gross of green spectacles. But the Trust Magnate, the
type of all that is business-like, really does have to buy
a gross of rose-coloured spectacles. To see everything
pink and pretty is really a necessity of his nonsensical
existence. Hence we find that in America, the home of
this kind of colossal commerce and combination, practically all their strange sects agree about this strange philosophy of Optimism. Everybody is educated in a sort

of permanent ethic of unmeaning hopefulness, or, as the idiom of the civilization goes, the duty of "being as cheerful as the cheerfullest man in sight." There is a great deal in the American character that really does cheer the soul of man by spirit and example; a great deal of social courage in the way of the self-organization of the populace; a great deal of instinctive consideration of men as men; a great deal of honourable pride in hard work; a certain absence of fundamental cynicism; a certain presence of casual confidence in strangers. But though I really like Americans myself, I think their cheerfulness is the most dismal thing about them.

At least it has become a dismal thing, in so far as it no longer refers to the old realities of democracy, but rather to the new unrealities of plutocracy and publicity. It is a proverb that this kind of Yankee is considered very wide-awake. But what is now the matter with him is that he is asleep and dreaming; his wealth is such stuff as dreams are made of, and his little life is rounded with a slump. But the same criticism applies to English Business Government, and generally to that cosmopolitan business Government which now rules us all. Where it differs from a true system of Property, the real condition of Hormatcy to which some give the name of Distributism, is in the simple fact that Distributism is not a dream. It is a project, which may or may not be found practicable by particular people at a particular time.

But when it is established, its fundamental facts, like the land or the family, are not affected by what other people say about them. They do not vanish as the result of a rumour or roll away like clouds because somebody relaxes the rigid strain of being optimistic about them. They have a life of their own, and they go on of themselves; and when they are in vigour, there is a free and happy society; in which men are liberated from the horrible slavery of smiling.

VII. THE CASE FOR MAIN STREET

I AM on the side of Main Street in the main. I mean by the statement, not that I prefer Main Street as it is to Main Street as it ought to be, but that I prefer even Main Street as it is to the views of those who think it ought not to be. I mean that if I were driven to the awful—nay, ghastly—alternative of choosing between its critics and itself, I should prefer that it should remain itself. If I were absolutely forced to choose between being a Methodist real estate agent in Gopher Prairie or being an artist, anarchist and atheist in Greenwich Village, I should (in the stern spirit of one bracing himself to terrible renunciations and the facing of a dreadful doom) decide to be a real estate agent. And I should say this even with every sympathy for the artist, because simple people may be at the beginning of beauty, whereas sophisticated people have come to the end of beauty and the end of everything. But when it comes to describing the positive virtues of Main Street, I am in a difficulty, because Main Streeters are unconscious of their virtues. That is the greatest of all their virtues.

There is a difficulty in this sort of international explanation. If I suggest even vaguely that Gopher Prairie is a virtuous village I can see Mr. Sinclair Lewis watching me with irony kindling in his eye and ready to launch the most brilliant wit and blasting satire for my extinction. But the truth is that he and I not only mean two different things by the word "virtuous," but we mean two different things by the word "village." Nothing marks as more absolute the abyss of the Atlantic than the colour and connotation of the word "village." There is no such thing in England, let alone Europe, as a Puritan village. There is such a thing as a Pagan village.

The penetrating pen of the author of *The Spoon River Anthology* noted down as one of the few good points in that rather unpleasing community that the Irish priest had helped those who sought to save the village from the bleak bigotry of "village morality." In that sense there is no such thing in England as village morality. In that sense there is very little except village immorality. Yet Mr. Lee Masters or Mr. Sinclair Lewis, coming into an English village, would instantly feel the virtues of a pagan village. They would feel a freedom, a good nature, a toleration of the village drunkard and the village idiot. I feel bound, on my side, to see and salute the virtues of a Puritan village. I can see for myself that it is not only Puritan, but also, in the real sense, Republican.

Men imagine their own virtues much more universal than they really are. If the foreigner tells them they are absent from foreign countries, they revolt into a curious error. With the very paradox of humility, they suppose the foreigners to be specially vicious, rather than suppose themselves to be specially virtuous. As I say, it is a beautiful innocence in human nature, but it leads to some very ugly imaginations about human beings. If a Norman peasant works hard, he thinks little of hard work. He even takes hard work lightly. But if he is told that Neapolitan peasants work less hard, he cannot take that lightly, and he generally imagines that the Neapolitans are much lazier than they are.

So it is with the American, if he is congratulated by the Englishman on the very real elements of equality and fraternity that are instantly felt by a man entering America. It is strictly true that an Englishman of any liberality does feel a certain kind of fresh air, from which a certain kind of smell has departed, and the thing that has vanished is snobbishness. But the American will be wildly wrong if he infers from this that the atmosphere of England is merely snobbish. The atmosphere of England is an extremly subtle blend of liberty and aristocracy and a universal belief in courtesy, with a sort of by-product of snobbishness; but a by-product which smells to heaven. But the American says to himself, "What snobs these people must be if they think it odd that folks should be friendly." And he immediately makes a picture of feudal England which is no more like

England than William the Conqueror in a waxwork show is like George V taking tea in the drawing-room.

It is always easier to explain these complex cross-purposes by concrete cases. I found an exact illustration of what I really like in America. It occurred in a country town where there is a college or university in which I had just lectured. One of the professors was kind enough to say that he liked my line of argument and that it had contained one point that had not occurred to him before. A minute or two later, as I was standing waiting outside the hall, the same professor's chauffeur came up to me in exactly the same manner and said almost exactly the same thing. He said he agreed upon that particular point, but was doubtful upon some other point of controversy. There was absolutely no difference between the tone and gesture and bodily carriage of the professor and his servant. Neither was aggressive; neither was apologetic; neither thought it anything but natural to say something that had just come into his head.

That is what I like in America. That is what is nearly impossible in England. But the trouble is this: that if I say that such an incident in England would be impossible, crowds of untravelled Americans will instantly make up pictures of an arrogant aristocratic England which would be far more impossible. Many might be left with a vague idea that English chauffeurs are not admitted to lectures; or that English chauffeurs cannot read or write and are incapable of understanding lectures; or that English chauffeurs are silent out of terror of their haughty and high-born masters; or that English gentlemen strut about like Prussian Junkers, twirling military moustaches and shouting military orders to miserable chauffeurs.

Nothing of this sort could possibly happen; any more than the other thing could happen. I know exactly what would happen. It is a matter of tone; of social atmosphere; of something that can generally be better conveyed by a novelist than an essayist. Most probably the lady of the house, radiantly receiving the lecturer, might even notice the presence of the chauffeur, or the butler or the gamekeeper or the gardener or some other upper servant. And she would very probably say, with a curious sort of foggy affection in her mind, "Wiggins will take care of you. I do hope you will be comfortable." Then with a sort of running up the scale of laughter, "Wiggins went to your lecture. Wiggins reads quite a lot of books"; all with a curious warmth of pride in her tone, as if she owned the learned pig or the calculating horse or some quite exceptional animal of whom she was rather fond. And Wiggins would at first look sheepish, as if he had been caught stealing books from the library, and grin in an apologetic but speechless manner. And only afterwards when you had agreed with Wiggins about a hundred times that it was a fine day, might he begin to make fragmentary human noises, and you might learn something of what he thought of the lecture. But, anyhow, that is the difference. There is no question, in the ordinary sense, of being overbearing or brutal with such servants. One of the very first things that the small squire will be taught at the age of six is the sacred necessity of being polite to Wiggins. But he will never be the equal of Wiggins; and Wiggins will never act as if he were. That they should both comment on a strange gentleman's lecture, independently, simultaneously, spontaneously, in the same tone and at the same time—that is what does not happen in England and that is what does happen in America.

To say that America is more democratic lets loose a wild confusion of tongues. For democracy, strictly speaking, does not mean ease or equality or comradeship among the people. It means direct government by the people. Now government by the people is a devilish difficult thing to establish at all, at least in a modern complicated industrial State. It is supposed to exist in America; for that matter, it is supposed to exist in England; but its existence can be very easily doubted or disputed anywhere. It is not of the political conception of popular rule that I am talking just now. What exists in America is not democracy, which may or may not be possible. It is equality, which was always supposed to be much more impossible. It is not impossible. As an atmosphere, but an actual atmosphere, the sense of social equality (or if you prefer the phrase, the absence of rank) does exist in America, as it does not exist in Europe. It is not an impossibility; it is not a possibility; it is a positive fact. It exists to show that Jefferson did something, as Islam exists to show that Mahomet did something. It is mixed up with all sorts of abuses and abominations, like other human achievements; but it is achieved.

I will mention another incident which illustrates another aspect of the same thing. It illustrates something impossible in England and possible in America; but the moral is so much more subtle that it might not be understood by Americans any more than by Englishmen. It is only fair to say that it occurred in a town with no university, a place the reverse of academic. It may be that the man I met was only a freak or adventurer, but I do not think so. Anyhow, I have never met such a freak or had such an adventure in any other land, least of all in my own land. He seemed to think it was quite natural and, if the American reader thinks it was nothing except trivial, my point about the difference is proved.

I had come out of my hotel and was walking, I trust inoffensively, down the street, when a young man stopped and spoke to me. He was shabby, not so shabby

as I was, but with that indescribably genuine air sug-
gesting that his shabbiness was due to poverty and not
like mine, to natural inefficiency. He was not obtrusive
or vulgar; he had a sharp, refined face; he spoke quite
quietly and in my own beloved island would have been
in some danger of being removed as a lunatic. He said,
"Pardon me. May I ask if you are one of our local
statesmen?"

I replied politely that I was not one of his local statesmen. I added that if his locality possessed any statesmen, it was more fortunate than most localities are just
now. He replied:

"Pardon my curiosity, but something about your appearance suggested to me that you must be a statesman
—or else a writer."

This shaft struck nearer home, and I admitted that I
had once or twice written things. At this he got quite
excited and said, "I also am a writer"; and produced
sheafs of papers from his pocket, including press cuttings
presumably appreciative of what he wrote. I stood looking through them with blear-eyed urbanity, and we remained thus in conference in the middle of the street,
holding up the traffic as it were, while the endless local
processions of gangsters or oil magnates streamed or
struggled past us. Then he asked, still with a certain
delicacy, whether I would mind telling him what sort of
things I wrote. I replied vaguely that I had written a lot

of rather different things, from shockers and murder mysteries to some little trifles on topics of theology and philosophy.

He held up his hand suddenly, like a traffic signal, and said, "That's my subject!"

Then he dived again into the sheaf of papers and brought out a photograph of an old man with a very big beard and very big feet, in sandals, walking in the sunlight; a sort of parody of Walt Whitman.

"If you want any philosophy," said my mad friend confidentially, tapping the photograph and talking like a man recommending a tobacconist, "if ever you want any philosophy, that's the man. He lives at Apocalypse Villa on Revelation Hill," or some such address.

I was ashamed of my lack of enthusiasm; one glance at the venerable humbug in the photograph had told me, child of an older and wearier civilization, what sort of philosophy I should get from him. Doubtless there are hundreds like him in all countries, if a few more thousands like him in that country; and it may be that there are thousands like his conversational admirer. He concluded with a truly human touch, by producing a photograph of his son in uniform, a student at West Point. But I was not at that moment thinking of what was curious about him. I was thinking of something much more curious about myself. And I suddenly saw, in a lightning-flash not perhaps to be recovered, what I really like in America—and even in Main Street.

I am not saying anything here about what I like in England. I leave it to be understood how massive and manifold are the great qualities that I should praise in my own house and people; the largesse, the uncommanded charity, the understanding of loneliness and liberty, the humour and the deep soil from which the poets sprang. But there is in the English atmosphere a certain evil, and the mere absence of that atmosphere, when I realized it, startled me like a strange smell. I suddenly remembered, like something a thousand miles away, that if a shabby man had begun to talk to me like that in Fleet Street, I should not even have thought he was a lunatic; I should have thought nothing so noble. I should have thought, I should have been unable to prevent myself from thinking, that he wanted me to give or lend him money.

When I remembered those shamefaced approaches there fell on me from afar the shame that lies heavier on the rich than the poor, and heavier on the lender than the borrower. I remembered a sordid something, and I remembered that I had not remembered it before. A thousand things had crossed my mind while conversing with that amiable lunatic in the street, but it had never even crossed my mind that he merely wanted money. It had never crossed my mind, and it had never crossed his mind. He did not know that there is an atmosphere where such sudden buttonholings are suspect. He did not want anything out of me, except the time and attention of a total stranger; and he never so much as thought that I could think he did.

What could be more natural than telling a total stranger in the street all about your favourite philosophy and your soldier son? He certainly made no attempt to draw any practical advantage from that extraordinary conversation; and I do not think it was ever in his mind. Nor, in that place and time, was it in my mind. And that fact means something if it were rightly studied; something about a social atmosphere that has never been rightly named. There had gone completely out of my head the memory of a certain sort of harassed and humiliated relation of rich and poor. Every genuine Englishman will know what I mean. Every truthful Englishman will agree with what I say.

Now this note, though it be only negative, is very queer; is on the face of it a paradox. There is much more talking about money in America than in England; there is any amount of worrying about money, groping for money, grabbing, stealing and swindling for money in America and everywhere else. A man would be likely enough to stop me in that street to sell me a gold brick or a vanishing oil field; I would not put it past him, in the American phrase, to stick me up for any blackguard form of blackmail or bribery. All those crude forms of crime were potentially there, but there was something that was not there. It was a sort of uncomfortable convention, painfully familiar to more stratified social systems, that the shabby man does not stop the more prosperous unless he is, if not a sort of blackmailer, at least a sort of beggar. That is really the bad side of inequality. It is rather worse when it is a sort of undefined or informal inequality; and the poor man sometimes spoke more freely when he was a slave.

These problems, indeed, can only be dealt with in paradoxes. Listening to the mere talk of Englishmen, a stranger might suppose that nobody ever thought about rank. Listening to the mere talk of Americans, a stranger might suppose that everybody always thought about money. But I believe these impressions are not only profoundly untrue, but pretty nearly the reverse of the truth. Lord Palmerston, when asked to define a gentleman, very shrewdly replied, "a man who never uses the word." Every Englishman knows that it is caddish to be always talking about being gentlemanly. But it is none the less true that the ideal thus protected from verbal vulgarization runs through all modern English history and is the cue to it. We might almost say that the romance of the gentleman has been the religion of the Englishman.

On the other hand, the ordinary American seems ready to talk about dollars to any stray stranger. But he is not always trying to get dollars out of the stray stranger. If he were, the whole social habit would very rapidly be abandoned. In some cases he talks for the sake of good fellowship. In some cases he talks for the sake of talking. Readers of Mr. Sinclair Lewis will remember that *The Man Who Knew Coolidge* did not exactly imitate the alleged silence of Coolidge. He talked through a whole book, and he talked a great deal about his business, which was, if I remember right, the furnishing of office fittings. But Mr. Lewis, though a realist, cannot entirely escape reality. A highly intelligent though perhaps unconscious instinct made him pay the poor traveller a very true though perhaps unintentional compliment. It will be remarked that, though *The Man Who Knew Coolidge* talks incessantly and interminably about selling the goods, he does not apparently sell any goods. Still less does he beg or borrow any money. He is an artist inspired by a sort of art for art's sake. He talks for the love of talking; which is something much more generous than the love of money.

That disinterested directness, that assumption that any American can talk to anybody else and talk about money as much as about anything else, is the key to my odd psychological experience in the street. That is why I did in some way feel at ease with the strange man in California, as I might not have felt at ease with a strange man in Camden Town. All nations naturally laugh at each other, and I can, of course, find much that strikes me as odd about that friendly footpad, with his private press cuttings and his photograph of a philosopher. Apparently he found much that was odd about me. He must have looked at me much as he would have looked at a hippopotamus passing placidly through his town, or he would hardly have so wantonly arrested me and accused me of being a statesman.

But, with all my English amusement at his American abruptness, I can see that there was in it a great quality of truth and candour and that my very acceptance of it was an unconscious tribute to something unspoiled and healthy in his strange sociability. It is the breath of something not quite broken or stifled even by the brutalities and trickeries of all that materialism which is the burden of America and the whole modern world; a memory of brotherhood, an assumption of manhood, a sort of good and golden simplicity and spontaneity that recalls even yet the ancient visions of Atlantis as a sort of Utopia and the hope that filled the founding of the Western republics; something not altogether unworthy of that golden Californian air. For the golden age only comes to men when they have, if only for a moment, forgotten gold.

There are men in Main Street, there are men in America, who can forget money even when they are talking about money. They are not expecting money;

they are not asking for money; they are not cadging for money. They are talking about money. It is their subject but not their object. This is their great virtue and I hasten to veil it from them, for it is not good for men to know how good they are.

VIII. THEY ARE ALL PURITANS

THERE is supposed to be a sort of civil war raging in America, in the literary sense, between the Puritans and the Anti-Puritans. In this case, obviously, we cannot say between the Puritans and the Cavaliers; for the active Anti-Puritans are men like Sinclair Lewis and Mr. Mencken, whose one remaining link with the Republic is probably their disinclination to draw swords and die for the King. But they can be called the Puritans and the Anti-Puritans, and a stranger from England or Europe, after studying the two factions, will be tempted to make a certain assertion about them both. At least I am tempted to make it though I recognize that it is a simplification and perhaps an oversimplification. I am tempted to say that they are all Puritans, especially the Anti-Puritans.

Of course, there are the usual exceptions and marginal differences and debates about definition. The religion that remains in the ruck of American villages doubtless differs from the origins from which its sects arose. It is not pure Puritanism. It is something rather impure that is the only practical product of Puritanism. It might be called, in the more general sense, Prohibitionism. But then pure Puritanism did not exist for more than a generation or two of unnatural exaltation and exclusion, in the course of which it did some extraordinary things, outside the normal, and certainly outside the nineteenth-century Nonconformity.

The Puritan substituted a God who wished to damn people for a God who wished to save them. He pushed the Parliament to oppose the King and then wrecked the Parliament in order to kill the King. He revived the barbaric butchery of all prisoners of war, in the case of the Calvinist ministers after the defeat of Montrose. He created the Scottish Sabbath, compared with which the Jewish Sabbath is jolly. But every man has a sane spot somewhere; and he was not a teetotaller.

The particular scruples of the modern Puritan differ from the particular scruples of the original Puritan, save in the essential point that both have always been at once violent and trivial. The essential of the Puritan mood is the misdirection of moral anger. It is having righteous indignation about the wrong thing. That the new Puritans have added some new wrong things to the old heretical heritage of wrong things does not alter the essential qualification: that they take care to be wrong about what they think wrong.

To the old vices of gambling and gambolling they have added the vice of beer drinking; but whether we call the new amalgam Puritanism or something else, it exists and we must call it something. The English name given in my youth was the Nonconformist Conscience, but in England it is dead, while in America it is still considerably alive. It is in this sense that I say that the Anti-Puritans are Puritans; are almost more Puritan than the Puritans. Sinclair Lewis is a Puritan. The ordinary detached freethinker or freelance, like Walter Lippmann, is a Puritan. The late James Huneker was a Puritan. Mr. Mencken is a Puritan. They are all Puritans.

What I mean is this: between the two extremes of Mrs. Carrie Nation smashing saloons with axes and the Bohemian in Greenwich Village sipping strange culture with absinthe, there are of course a thousand shades of common sense or common senselessness. There is every sort of sane American citizen between the mad Puritan and the mad Pagan. But from my own standpoint, which is neither Puritan nor Pagan, there is one rather curious thing that is common to them all. For instance, one kind of man will say in effect, "I don't believe a man can be a good citizen unless he's a good Christian, and the Bible that was good enough for my mother is good enough for me. I don't say I've never taken a drink, but I don't allow it in my house and I'd give anything to save my sons from gambling."

Then there is a second sort of man who will say, "I'm afraid I can't believe in any creed myself, though of course I've a great respect for Christ and good Christians. It's all very well for them; but naturally I don't go

in for being a saint; I take a drink from time to time
though not as a habit, and I'm not above a game of
poker."

Then we have the type of man who says more impa-
tiently, "Oh, these Christians are too good for this
world, or they pretend to be, though lots of them are
dirty hypocrites and drink on the sly. They aren't so
darned Christian when you come to know them. I make
no pretences. Craps and whisky and this world's good
enough for me."

Next to him we have a wilder specimen who says,
"Christianity's been nothing but a blasted blight on all
the fun and freedom of humanity. I'm not ashamed of
saying, 'Eat and drink, for tomorrow you die.' All the
Christian ever says is, 'Don't drink and hardly eat, for
tomorrow you're damned.' You read what Mencken
says about the ministers who want to cut out gambling,
etc." Then of course there is the more logical and philosophical culmination of the same philosophy, as in Mr.
Mencken himself.

Now there are any number of intelligent and kindly
and jolly people of all those shades of thought. But what
I remark about them is that they are all Puritans, at
least they are all what we call in England Nonconformists. They all have the exact but extraordinary Nonconformist scale of moral values. They all have the same
fixed but astounding notion of the nature of Christian-

ity. Some of them accept Christianity and therefore refuse wine or whisky or games of chance. Some of them
hesitate about Christianity and therefore hesitate about
wine or whisky or games of chance. Some of them reluctantly reject Christianity and therefore (almost reluctantly) accept wine and whisky and games of chance.
Some of them deliriously reject Christianity and therefore deliriously accept wine or whisky or games of
chance. But they all seem incurably convinced that
things like that are the main concern of religion. It is a
pretty safe bet that if any popular American author has
mentioned religion and morality at the beginning of a
paragraph, he will at least mention liquor before the end
of it. To a man of a different creed and culture the whole
thing is staggering. To such a stranger the Puritanism
of Mencken is more of a puzzle than the Puritanism of
Moody and Sankey.

Such a stranger however, should remember that
Americans have one great merit, which more than out-
balances all their morality. I mean that idealism and
Uplift and the Utmost for the Highest, and all the rest
of it does not do them so much harm as would be done
to another sort of society; to a more corrupt or cowardly
people; to a more sluggish or a more secretive race. They
not only have the virtue, but, what is even better, the
unconsciousness of the virtue. Anyhow, even when they
know they have it, they do not know that it is partic-

ularly virtuous; and it is so much out of the track of
their traditional moralizing, that I do not myself know
exactly how it is to be stated so as not to be misunderstood.

I might express it somewhat abruptly by saying that
most Americans are born drunk; and really require a
little wine or beer to sober them. They have a sort of
permanent intoxication from within; a sort of invisible
champagne which needs to be weighted and soothed
and supplemented by something corresponding to the
glass of port with which the English were accustomed
to conclude and settle their dinner. Americans do not
need drink to inspire them to do anything; though they
do sometimes, I think, need a little for the deeper and
more delicate purpose of teaching them how to do nothing.

An Englishman watching an American is sometimes
tempted to wonder, almost wildly, what he would be
like if he were drunk, when he is like this even when he
is sober; and there may be, I admit, concealed in this
consideration something like a psychological excuse for
Prohibition. For if the American did drink (and it may
be hinted that Americans sometimes do) I fear he
would not be drinking port or strong ale or any of these
solid drinks; but only whisky, which would have the
fearful effect of making him even more enterprising
than before. Nevertheless, although an Englishman can-

not help feeling this faint wonder at the sight of such auto-intoxicated activity, he will, if he is wise, recognize that it is connected with a real virtue, compared with which mere abstinence from alcohol might almost be called a vice.

I have already remarked that all Americans are Puritans, excepting those that are Catholics, but not excepting those that are atheists or anarchists or, more dangerous still, artists. The Pagans are Puritans; the enemies of Puritanism are Puritans; they prove it by the way in which they identify the last fads of Puritanism with the first principles of Christianity. The very fact that they think they can defy religion by drinking and smoking shows precisely what is the only religion they have ever found to defy.

But while their conscious Christianity is nearly always some such shallow business, about whether there are any cigarettes in the Bible, their unconscious Christianity is not shallow but very deep indeed. And it is bound up, curiously enough, with this curious careering energy, which may seem at first sight a mere selfish snatching at a career. But there is something else in it; something of a sort of simplicity which many an Englishman would find too simple to understand.

I once wrote a sort of nonsense essay, urging that the saint or the true Christian ought to find nothing but childlike enthusiasm in running after his hat. The

American citizen would really, with an excitement bordering on enthusiasm, run after his hat. The English gentleman would be much more annoyed at having to run after his hat; indeed it is the whole paradox of that strange being; that he could never be persuaded that it is more sensible to run after a hat he does want than after a ball he doesn't want. The point is that the American would really be thinking about his hat, and not about the rest of his appearance. The mere flight of the hat would carry all the rest of him with it, without any sort of self-consciousness; without self-importance and without self-contempt. He often runs after things that are much less harmless than his hat. He sometimes runs after things that are not his at all. But in brigandage, in murder and even in business, there is this touch of innocence: the absence of the paralysis of pride. Even what is called hustle has that unconscious goodness about it that the hustler is not ashamed of being in a hurry.

I fear it will be rejected as a paradox, rather than accepted as a compliment, if I say that even wild American reporters out for a story have a strange link with Christian humility. But it is amusing to notice, even in their appearance in popular literature, such as the crime stories with which I cram my pockets, how free they are from the sophisticated self-consciousness of more respectable heathens. We can generally guess the secret ideal of a nation from the conventional hero of novel. We all know the conventions required to make the English hero conventional. One of the first is that he should be comfortable even when he is uncomfortable. When perched upon the breaking bridge above the yawning chasm, he shows he is an English hero by smoking a cigarette, with a slightly bored expression, or even perhaps (with a polite gesture) yawning, like the chasm.

But the Americans do not really admire boredom, even in a martyr at the point of death. They do really admire excitement, even in a man surrounded by all the comforts of life. The young hero, who is often a young reporter, in my favourite American romances, is excited all the time; he is excited by everything or by anything. A pin or a postage stamp will alike send him flying out of his seat; a taunt or a telegram will equally catapult him across the room; the mention of a job will hurl him out of the window; the chance of a "scoop" will send him out through the skylight. The editor likes him for it; the heroine likes him for it, and I will frankly confess that I like him for it.

I am myself of the very opposite national temper and tradition, and no opportunities of writing for any paper will propel me through even the most conveniently placed skylights or windows. But the more meditative habit may sometimes be used to cultivate a sense of justice. And I recognize in that young lunatic a streak of sincerity and singlemindedness and thoughtlessness about appearances, which I think may yet hurl him to some wild country not far from the Kingdom of Heaven.

IX. SKYSCRAPERS

A SKYSCRAPER is an imaginative name; but then it is an imaginary thing. Nobody notices that it does not exist. The name was originally a very fine example of the American lie; which is the recognized form of the American joke. Everybody has forgotten the joke, but continues to use the name, and that is in itself an interesting example of the power of the modern mind of inhabiting an imaginary world almost without knowing it; of moving in a sort of dream amid the assumptions of a land of unreason. The title of the skyscraper is quite a good legend or fable; it belongs to the same world as the Man in the Moon or the Sultan who is brother of the Sun and Stars. But the men who used these legendary terms knew that they were legendary; or even if they thought they were true, did not think they were self-evident. But modern language, especially American language, is packed with exaggerations to which men have grown accustomed; exaggerations that no longer sound exaggerative. It is full of wild tales that have grown tame.

The tale of the first skyscraper, the Tower of Babel, has not grown entirely tame. One of the strongest arguments for a sacred and separate religious enclosure in human life is that some things are thereby saved from a certain sort of familiarity which rapidly obliterates the beauty and wonder of ordinary things. Men may make a hundred jokes about the Tower of Babel; and a man could still make an epic about it. But of the hundred million human beings who say the word "skyscraper" every day, there are probably very few indeed who remember that when the word was first used, it was a sort of fantastic poem. One result of this overstimulation, and consequent staleness of the imagination, is the fact that those who live among all these faded fancies hardly know a fact when they see it. Nothing will induce them to believe, for instance, that the Distributist ideal is the most real and even realistic of all ideals; that it is concerned with the most solid sort of facts. They know it is really impossible to scrape the sky with a spire; but they use it as a form of speech. But when we say that it is possible to scrape the earth with a spade, they think it is a fairytale.

It is another irony that men first discovered that they could build skyscrapers, at the same moment as they discovered that there was no such thing as the sky. Savages and simple peoples have dreamed of castles in the clouds or gods riding the tempest; but the same men who discovered that they could pierce the vault of space with turrets and towering engines also realized that there was nothing to be found there. Henceforward even the builders of the Tower of Babel would not be blasphe-mously scaling heaven. They would be, strictly speaking, only falling, falling and falling, as in the nightmare of Lucretius, into a bottomless void. This also may partly explain the rapidity with which the imaginative element in such megalomaniac phraseology fades from the very words. If the skyscraper is a forgotten myth, it is not only because the scraper is mythical, but because the sky is mythical too. Of the things of which our fathers made legends and epics, we can only make jests. It is true that there are artistic effects of the skyscraper, about which solemn things can be written; as about any powerful and extreme exercise of the mysterious energy of man. But even these modern meditations, at their best, seem to me to have a curious quality of detachment from humanity; a quality that is not quite sane. It will be constantly said, for instance, that looking down from the top of a skyscaper, a man sees a marvellous map of the city or the world, flattened out into mathematical meas-urements and proportions, and reducing men to dots like a dust of atoms. But that power of distance is an illusion; quite as much of an illusion as the beauty of blue hills, and far less symbolically true. Men are not dots or atoms, though a man were to look at them from the top of a pagoda of skyscrapers; and it is not good for him to fall into the way of thinking that they are. It has been felt often enough, of course, long before skyscrapers were dreamed of; and it has been expressed far more finely than the moderns express it. Shakespeare saw the vision from the top of Shakespeare's Cliff; but he knew his business, and described it through the mouth of a madman. For nearly everybody in the play of King Lear is more or less mad.

There is one lesson to be learnt from skyscrapers, which just now is very vital—or rather very deadly. It illustrates that huge inhuman anomaly of modern men being cut off from the very earth. It is connected with what I have said about the impossibility of scraping the sky and the possibility of scraping the soil. A perfect parallel of our whole argument might be offered, in a story of the men in the lower flats of a skyscraper starting to starve out the men in the higher ones. The men in the higher ones would have every advantage of what are called modern improvements and conveniences; light and ventilation and telephones and hot and cold water— until they were cut off at the main. But they could not devour telephone wires, and might even be averse from eating soap; and unless they could grow a kitchen-garden in a window-box, they would presumably die or surrender. A fine American epic might be written about the battle in the big hotel, with its multitudinous cells for its swarming bees. It might describe the exciting battle for the elevators; the war of the nameless and numberless guests, known only by their numbers. It might describe the gallant sally of 55783, who succeeded in seizing and working the thirty-second lift; the heroic conduct of 62017, in bringing up an armful of yams and sweet potatoes by the fire-escape; of the deathless deeds of 65991, whose name, or rather number, will resound for ever in history. It would be great fun; and it would illustrate the Distributist argument.

One word should emphatically be added. It is a slander on America to call it a land of skyscrapers. It is a gross injustice to Americans to suppose that most of them live in large hotels. An enormous number of them live in little wooden houses, looking rather like dolls'-houses, each with a porch in front; and they are immeasurably happier and better than anybody in the very biggest hotel; and perhaps happiest of all in the fact that nobody has ever heard of them.

X. AND WHAT ABOUT THE QUAKERS?

THE Americans have established a Thanksgiving Day to celebrate the fact that the Pilgrim Fathers reached America. The English might very well establish another Thanksgiving Day; to celebrate the happy fact that the Pilgrim Fathers left England. I know that this is still regarded as a historical heresy, by those who have long ceased to worry about a religious heresy. For while these persons still insist that the Pilgrim Fathers were champions of religious liberty, nothing is more certain than the fact that an ordinary modern liberal, sailing with them, would have found no liberty, and would have intensely disliked almost all that he found of religion. Even Thanksgiving Day itself, though it is now kept in a most kindly and charming fashion by numbers of quite liberal and large-minded Americans, was originally intended, I believe, as a sort of iconoclastic expedient for destroying the celebration of Christmas. The Puritans everywhere had a curious and rabid dislike of Christmas; which does not encourage me, for one, to develop a special and spiritual fervour for Puritanism. Oddly enough, however, the Puritan tradition in America has always celebrated Thanksgiving Day by often eliminating the Christmas Pudding, but preserving the Christmas Turkey. I do not know why, unless the very name of Turkey reminded them of the Prophet of Islam, who was also the first Prophet of Prohibition.

It is not, however, in connexion with either Thanksgiving Day or Christmas Day, that I recur for a moment to the somewhat controversial question of the Pilgrim Fathers. It is merely to note anew that there has always seemed to me too much emphasis on the Pilgrim Fathers, as compared with many others who were at least as truly Fathers of the Republic. There has certainly been in recent times a considerable combination between Puritanism and Publicity. The Puritans may not always have approved of the stage; but for all that they got a great deal of the limelight. Somebody managed to make the *Mayflower* as legendary as the Ark or the Argo; indeed, it is legendary in more ways than one, so far as the aim and atmosphere of the expedition are concerned. But I doubt whether most people even know the names of the ships in which many of the other devoted or heroic colonists of America sailed; I, for one, most certainly do not. I will not insist especially on the very noble example of Lord Baltimore and the founders of the State of Maryland; who established the first system of religious toleration in history; for there I might be accused of favouring my own religious sympathies and ideas. But I am at least detached and impartial in the subsequent and somewhat similar story of the founding of the State of Pennsylvania. And whatever ship brought the great Quakers to that settlement has a rather better right than the *Mayflower* to be called, in the language of Mr. Ford, a Peace Ship.

These reflections occurred to me when I was recently standing in the city of Philadelphia; on which looks down the great statue of William Penn, whose unmarked grave lies a mile or two from my own house at home. And it struck me as very strange that all the millions of men, with modern humanitarian sympathies, have said so little of the immense superiority of that intellectual and spiritual leader to the clamorously advertised Calvinists of the *Mayflower*. I gravely fear that a great many of them do not even see much difference between the two. Among the most curious of all curiosities of literature, or of legend, I have actually heard a sort of romantic rumour (which I have never been able either to trace or test) that portions of the timber of the *Mayflower* were found in some strange way attached to the old Quaker meeting-house that stands beside Penn's grave. I cannot imagine what the story could possibly mean; or how the incident can possibly be supposed to have come about; unless indeed some enthusiastic American globe-trotter merely threw fragments of *Mayflower* furniture (said to be rather suspiciously common in the States) at any house that had any connexion with any founder of any American State. Anyhow, he might just as well have said that Sir Walter Raleigh sailed in the *Mayflower* as connect William Penn and his people with the fanaticism that filled that famous vessel. He might as well have hung the first Calvinistic meeting-house with rosaries and relics and scapularies, belonging to the Catholic Calverts, as pretend to have patched up the house of the first Friends with the relics of their mortal enemies and persecutors, the old Puritans. An American Puritan in the seventeenth century would have regarded a Quaker very much as an American Puritan in the twentieth century would regard a Bolshevist. And though Bolshevists are supposed to be fierce and Quakers were supposed to be meek, they were at least alike in this; they were what modern America would call Radical; in the sense of going to the real root of the question, and answering it rightly or wrongly. In short, they were really Fundamentalists; and most Fundamentalists are not Fundamentalists. For whatever we think of the thing now called Fundamentalism, it is not fundamental. It is not particularly fundamental to throw a big Bible at people's heads (or rather a particular translation of the Bible, with a lot of books left out as Apocrypha) any more than to throw the Encyclopædia Britannica or the Institutes of Calvin. Even if it be a truth, it is not a first principle. But it is fundamental, and it is a first principle, right or wrong, to go back as William Penn did to the doctrine of the Inner Light.

For William Penn really was a great man and not merely a seventeenth-century sectarian; his thoughts, whether we think with him or no, have a meaning in the twentieth-century or any century; and he founded something much larger than Pennsylvania and much greater than Philadelphia; a faith that has not yet failed.

I think I know why Penn has been thrown into the shade by the Pilgrim Fathers. It was his politics; and for some they are still a dreadful secret. I was once asked by some worthy modern pacifists, of the Nonconformist culture, to lecture on something in one of the oldest meeting-houses of the Society of Friends. I agreed to lecture upon William Penn; and with secret and malignant joy drew up an elaborate plan for a eulogium on that Quaker hero. I set myself specially to express boundless admiration for all those parts of his life and opinion which his modern Puritan admirers do not admire. I proposed to praise extravagantly his loyal and devoted sympathy with the House of Stuart. I intended to point out eagerly, how worthy he was of the gracious and glorious friendship of a man like Charles the Second. I meant to rub in every detail of his diplomatic and political support of the admirable political designs of James the Second. I intended to insist on the intellectual amity, almost amounting to intellectual alliance, which so often bound him to Cavaliers and even to Catholics. In short, it was my evil intention to praise him for everything for which Macaulay blamed him. Then, I thought, when I have explained how intimately identified was Penn with the Royalists, and especially with the Papists—then surely all the Nonconformist ministers would be frightfully pleased. Then should I be acclaimed and admired by all the modern Puritans for my perfect understanding of the great seventeenth-century sectary. Then should I become the idol of all the people who glorify the Pilgrim Fathers and talk enthusiastically about the *Mayflower*. Then it would be admitted that I also was a grand grim old Puritan, like all the rest of them. Unfortunately, I fancy I must have boasted of my intention, and some rumour of it must have reached them. For I received at the eleventh hour a hurried request to give a lecture on Dickens. And from this we may learn that, if Dickens was an enemy of the Puritans, he was not so much of an enemy as Penn.

XI. ABRAHAM LINCOLN IN LONDON

SOME years ago, I remember, there was a considerable row in England about a statue of Abraham Lincoln, presumably proposed as a sort of compliment to America. It was not the statue which now stands in London, but one which was considered less complimentary. There were the usual disputes in the newspapers and the clubs, and even in the streets, similar to those which raged round Mr. Epstein's effigy of Rima. But there was, at any rate to my mind, a very vital difference between the cases. Rima was already an artistic product in literature before she became any sort of product in art. And it was at least reasonable to maintain that the Rima of art was not even close enough to be a caricature of the Rima of literature. Ugliness of a kind may be a legitimate element in art, but it was not a particularly characteristic element of Hudson's art. An innovator in sculpture may be entitled to call new and abnormal monsters out of the native rock, but it would seem that they should be nameless as well as new. But if a sculptor were called upon to carve a medallion of Jane Austen in Winchester Cathedral, it seems arguable that the Dean and Chapter would have some right to complain if he carefully followed the cranial lines of Pithecanthropus or ornamented the lady with enormous tusks and claws. If even the most original of the modern artists were called upon to design a monument of Miss Mitford to stand in the modest market-place of Our Village, his spirited design of a howling ape partly devoured by an alligator might give ground for criticism other than the strictly æsthetic. But if there really is a new anarchic artist who can create out of nothing a new abnormal monster, if there is an angle of artistic attack that could startle us with something utterly crude and yet creative, if there is an energy to be drawn from unfamiliar ugliness, and some style that shall be uncouth to the point of being uncanny, then I think that such a monstrosity would really be the best possible monument for Abraham Lincoln in London.

I was once concerned in a sort of controversy on the subject of Abraham Lincoln, in which I defended him from the charges of total abstinence, respectability, gentility, and the Anglo-Saxon spirit. As I explained at the time, I am a great admirer of Abraham Lincoln, but I am not an admirer of his admirers. I am not an admirer of the causes or the grounds or the spirit of their admiration. Perhaps I could best express my meaning by saying that, in the old original sense, it is not admiration at all. To admire is to wonder, and to wonder is to wonder at something strange. And no Englishman has even begun to appreciate Abraham Lincoln, who has not begun by wondering at so utterly strange a stranger. If his statue is to stand in London, it ought to be the statue of a stranger; nay, almost of a strange animal. The statue ought to strike us with the same sensation as that of meeting a grizzly bear in the Green Park or a bison in Bayswater. The starkest chasms, the most abrupt angles, of advanced sculpture could hardly do justice to the abyss that separates his type from ours. He was a great man, like Confucius, and a good man, like Uncle Remus; but he represented things as remote as their black and yellow races. He was no more an Anglo-Saxon than an Anglo-Indian; it would be rather more rational to compare him to a Red Indian. But, in truth, he was something to which the most staggering statuary could not do justice; something so separated from England that new planes and new dimensions of art would be needed to express the difference and the distance. He was an American.

Whilst I was in America, I often lingered in small towns and wayside places; and in a curious and almost creepy fashion the great presence of Abraham Lincoln continually grew upon me. I think it is necessary to linger a little in America, and especially in what many would call the most uninteresting or unpleasing parts of America, before this strong sense of a strange kind of greatness can grow upon the soul. What I mean is something quite indescribable, and I shall, of course, imme-

diately attempt to describe it. To begin with, I am
almost inclined to say that if the original unpopular
sculptor only made Lincoln ugly enough, he was probably all right. The complaints against the statue were
all to the effect that it was ugly; that the upper lip was
long and simian, that the hands hung large and loose,
that the attitude was that of an anthropoid ape. All
that sounds excellent. But I will not affirm that the
sculptor conveyed the secret of which I speak, for I am
by no means certain that it could be conveyed. Curiously enough, I feel as if it could be conveyed better by
landscape than by sculpture. It is the landscape of America that conveys it most vividly to me, especially all the
landscapes that would probably be most carefully
avoided by a landscape-painter.

The externals of the Middle West affect an Englishman as ugly, and yet ugliness is not exactly the point.
There are things in England that are quite as ugly or
even uglier. Rows of red brick villas in the suburbs of a
town in the Midlands are, one would suppose, as hideous
as human half-wittedness could invent or endure. But
they are different. They are complete; they are, in their
way, compact; rounded and finished with an effect that
may be prim or smug, but is not raw. The surroundings
of them are neat, if it be in a niggling fashion. But
American ugliness is not complete even as ugliness. It
is broken off short; it is ragged at the edges; even its

worthy objects have around them a sort of halo of refuse. Somebody said of the rugged and sardonic Dr. Temple, once Archbishop of Canterbury: "There are no polished corners in our Temple." There are polished corners in the English suburb, even if they are only varnished corners, vulgarly and greasily varnished corners. But there are no polished corners even in the great American cities, which are full of fine and stately classical buildings, not unworthy to be compared to temples. Nobody seems to mind the juxtaposition of unsightly things and important things. There is some deep difference of feeling about the need for completeness and harmony, and there is the same thing in the political and ethical life of the great Western nation. It was out of this landscape that the great President came, and one might almost trace a fanciful shadow of his figure in the thin trees and the stiff wooden pillars. A man of any imagination might look down these strange streets, with their framehouses filled with the latest conveniences and surrounded with the latest litter, till he could see approaching down the long perspective that long ungainly figure, with the preposterous stove-pipe hat and the rustic umbrella and deep melancholy eyes, the humour and the hard patience and the heart that fed upon hope deferred.

That is admiring Abraham Lincoln, and that is admiring America. It is when the stranger has absorbed all the strangeness, that he begins to understand a goodness that is not a mere imitation of the goodness of Europe or of England; something that an American writer has lately and very truly called "the folks ideal," expressed in an astonishing acceptance of the most incongruous people as "folks," a toleration of human beings in their shirt-sleeves, which is infinitely more distant and difficult than any pagan ranting about mere nakedness; an acceptance of humanity in obtuse angles and awkward attitudes, a thing altogether indescribable in English, except that it may be vaguely and faintly adumbrated in those two words "Abraham Lincoln."

Nowhere else in the world could a man of exactly that type have been a *great* man; he would at best have been a good man, generally derided as an exceedingly dowdy sort of dunce or failure. It is the real glory of that great democracy that it did draw out the capacities of such a man and turn him into a democratic leader; a demagogue who was not a dandy or a sham gentleman, or, for that matter, a real gentleman; not a cynic or one condescending to the common people, but one all the more great for a streak of something that was common. These are the sort of tasks that really await those who would reconcile the nations. But it will certainly never be done by putting up an ideal statue of old Abe, with a cricket-bat in one hand and an Anglo-Saxon grammar in the other, as a type of Character as formed by our English Public Schools.

XII. UNKNOWN AMERICA

It always mystifies me that, in the midst of the most absurd booming and boosting of Americanization, nobody ever says a word about the real virtues of America. It may perhaps appear less mysterious if I recall that, when England also had the misfortune to be the commercial leader of the world, nobody ever said a word about the real merits of England. People boasted of all sorts of trivial things, such as an Empire on which the sun never set, a large supply of coal, a map painted red, and a number of newspapers folded five or six times and filled with pompous articles, which were proudly compared with the mere leaflets of the boulevards, on which nothing was printed except what was thought worth printing. But they never boasted of the great and glorious things; they never boasted of bacon and eggs, or the creative originality of Chaucer, or the flowers in the front gardens of very poor people, or the admirable comic songs of the music-halls, which were, perhaps, the real literature of the English people in the nineteenth century. They had a grotesque energy that has hardly been heard since the Elizabethans, as in that beautiful but forgotten lyric in which a young lady named Jane is told that her "vocal vagaries have killed the canaries

and druv the gas back to the main"——an image of
startling force, as is the wild appeal of the poet in an
echo of the Song of Solomon:

O Wind from the South
Blow some mud in the mouth
Of Jane, Jane, Jane.

Yet I gravely doubt whether that exquisite English lyric
is included in any existing anthology, and I have looked
for it in vain in the Oxford Book of English Verse.

In the same way, I suppose, it was to be expected that
such boasts about America as commonly reach us across
the seas should be boasts about the things least worthy
of boasting. Gas and hot air, propelled by modern
machinery, travel much further than do the natural
smells and native air of any human province or habita-
tion. The gas, so far from being "druv back to the
main," is poured out easily to the ends of the earth;
and the Wind from the West has no difficulty in blowing a good deal of mud into the mouth, and out of the
mouth, of the typical modern publicity expert. But
while England is being, in this very paltry sense, Amer-
icanized, while London is being made to look like a bad
imitation of New York, nobody says anything at all
about the simpler and saner elements of American life,

which are almost as far from New York as from London. Nor is it merely a question of an atmosphere, which is always an indescribable thing. There are a considerable number of actual concrete facts in which America differs from England, and in which the serious moral advantage is with America. The queer thing is that these things are not only not admitted by the English, but are not even asserted by the Americans. They never figure at all in any of the controversies and recriminations of the two national systems. We still hear a certain amount of tired talk about being a Republic, which seems to mean no more than not calling a President by the title of a King; but we hear very little of the practical elements that really contribute to being a democracy. Some part of it is the fault of the English, because they always jumped to the conclusion that Americans were giving different names to the same thing; whereas there was much more danger of their giving the same name to different things. But the English have not always understood when it was really a case of different names for different things. When I used to read descriptions of the African element in American society, which referred to them as "coloured folks," I used to think it was a joke. I suppose it was a sort of jeering politeness to the Negro a sort of comic euphemism for "black." Anybody who goes to America sees at once that it is a correct and natural description, there being negroid people of every shade of brown or yellow or copper, who could no more be called black than they could be called peacock-green. Rather in the same way (and somewhat misled by Dickens in *Martin Chuzzlewit*) I always vaguely imagined that there was something a little priggish or pretentious about insisting on calling a servant "a help." But it is not so in the least. Helps are called helps because they are helps, and they are *not* in our sense servants. Often they are not notably of any different class from those whom they are helping; often they could really be better described as neighbours called in to help in the home. There are a great many small points of this sort in American social life, which most English people do not understand. And they are mostly connected with very virile and honourable American virtues, which most English people would do well to imitate. But it is only American vices that we are intent on imitating.

To take one concrete case: I believe a vast amount of what is really free and healthy in American life is due simply to the absence of the Game Laws. There is a space and atmosphere of adventure round boyhood, because there are no enclosures and the whole countryside is still largely treated as something with the promise of a wilderness. The poor as well as the rich have had "sport" with gun and fishing-rod, more freely in the old days than now, but still more freely in America than

England. What makes *Huckleberry Finn* one of the most glorious of all epics of boyhood is the indescribable sense that Huck really does potentially own the earth, that the world is all before him, and that America is itself one vast adventure story. I remember one verse of one rhyme I read in an American magazine in my childhood; I have no notion of the rest of the story, or the point of the story, and I dare say it had no point at all. But the words will jingle in my ear till I die, though they merely ran:

> There once was a bold nigger-boy,
> And that bold nigger-boy had a gun,
> And he wandered in comfort and joy
> In de woods where de waterfalls run.

It might be commended in passing to those who still taunt America because the Negroes were slaves, and are under the extraordinary delusion that our own white workers were free men. The nigger-boy was a good way ahead of most English workmen, even in having a gun; and if a poor man began to wander with his gun in the woods protected by the Game Laws, he certainly would not wander in comfort and joy.

Yet I have never heard anybody, on any side of the argument, American or English, so much as mention the words Game Laws. The real differences, whether they are English or American superiorities, never seem to figure in the international newspaper controversy. We are only called upon to admire the Americans for their hustle, their publicity, their commercial amalgamations. Nothing is ever said of the real republican virtues which still survive, in spite of the confused and corrupt politics of the Republic. Above all, we are especially taught to hail as the best thing in America what is certainly the worst thing in America. It is the horrible and repulsive thing called Optimism, which is akin in its metaphysics to Christian Science. That is, it is the direct denial both of Science and of Christianity, for Science rests wholly on the recognition of truth, and Christianity on the recognition of pain. This falsehood, which is but the fad of a few wealthy Americans, comes across the Atlantic in volumes of fog and smoke, as the vapour of one tall factory-chimney will stream far over a landscape, and carry no breath from the quiet and kindly cottages that lie at its foot. It is the final paradox that the best things do not travel, and yet we must travel to find them.

XIII. WHAT OF THE REPUBLIC?

STRANGE as it may seem, some are puzzled because I hate Americanization and do not hate America. I should have thought that I had earned some right to apply this obvious distinction to any foreign country, since I have consistently applied it to my own country. If the egoism is excusable, I am myself an Englishman (which some identify with an egoist) and I have done my best to praise and glorify a number of English things: English inns, English roads, English jokes and jokers; even to the point of praising the roads for being crooked or the humour for being Cockney; but I have invariably written, ever since I have written at all, against the cult of British Imperialism.

And when that perilous power and opportunity, which is given by wealth and worldly success, largely passed from the British Empire to the United States, I have applied exactly the same principle to the United States. I think that Imperialism is none the less Imperialism because it is spread by economic pressure or snobbish fashion rather than by conquest; indeed I have much more respect for the Empire that is spread by fighting than for the Empire that is spread by finance.

Anyhow, in both cases there is one constant factor:

that it is invariably the worst things that are spread. International imitation, like Imperialism, is nearly always servile in spirit; that is, it exhibits the taste of a slave even in the things to be imitated. The naked Negro wearing a top-hat is a criticism on the top-hat as well as on the Negro. And white men have succeeded in imposing black clothes upon the bodies of black men better than they have succeeded in imposing what are sometimes called white souls, or white standards of dignity and honour. It is an extraordinary thought: that among the thousand beautiful things that Europe has produced, from the Parthenon to the poetry of Keats, there is not one such thing that has been successfully copied; and the ugliest thing that Europe ever produced, which is its modern dress, has been copied by the whole world. What is true of races, like the white and the black, is equally true of nations, like the English and the American. A man can watch in every detail, day after day and year after year, the Americanization of London, and there will never come to him, even as a faint and far-off breath of any wind of the prairies, even a whisper of the real virtues of America.

The great virtue of America is that, in spite of industry and energy, in spite of progress and practical success, in spite of Edison and electricity, in spite of Ford and Fords, in spite of science and organization and enterprise and every evil work, America does really remain democratic; not perhaps in the literal sense of being a democracy, but in the moral sense of consisting of democrats. The citizens feel equal, even if they feel equally impotent. There may not be government of the people, by the people, for the people, but there is not government of the people, by the governing class, still less for the governing class. For anyone who knows anything of human history, with its heroic ideals and its prosaic disappointments, this really is and remains a remarkable achievement.

But it is impossible to get even a breath of this actual brotherhood without coming close to it, in its own plainest and even poorest habitations. The best American people are in the back-blocks and the by-streets; where even the rich Americans do not look for them, let alone the European travellers. It is in them that there endures an indescribable decency and security of soul; not poisoned by servility; not poisoned by pessimism. The good that is in them is naturally not known to globe-trotters, for it is not known to themselves. A Catholic priest said to me of some people in the Middle West: "They know nothing of their virtues and that must be pleasing to God." Main Street has been held up to the world as the worst thing in America. I think it is almost the best.

When we have allowed for this great American advantage we can speak equally plainly about the great

American disadvantage. I do not say that the wealth of America was a vice; it was merely a calamity. Also, whatever it was, it was. The calamity of riches has already been removed by the mercy of heaven. No; the real disadvantage of American civilization, the bad luck that balances the sincerity and simplicity of its main democratic design, lay in the relation between culture and creed. At the very beginning it got off on the wrong foot in the matter of faith and morals; and therefore its morals have been imperfect even when they were idealistic; we might say that they were the less perfect the more they were ideal. America had a great political idea, but it had a small religious idea. The spiritual vision was not wide enough for the breadth and variety of the brotherhood that was to be established among men.

America has never been quite normal. Anybody who has ever seen a normal populace will know what I mean at once, when I say that it is proved in the attitude toward drink and the attitude toward religion. As there is none of the sort of drink that sends men to sleep, so there is none of the sort of religion that gives men rest. The nation has numberless virile and independent farmers; yet they are not a normal peasantry. The farmers are often owners of solid and prosperous farms; yet it is not normal property. Something at once starved and strained, something too wide-awake to be fully human, belongs to the history of the Republic of the pioneers. It can be traced back, like everything else, to religion.

Somebody recently reproached me with living a double life; disguising myself as a Regular Guy and a citizen of Gopher Prairie, while I secretly kept another establishment and abandoned myself to dissipation as an English rustic, in the twenty-seven pubs of Auburn, sweetest village of the plain. In other words, he was puzzled because I had defended the manlier qualities of Main Street against the mere artificial anarchy of Greenwich Village, and yet declared (in a totally different connexion) that an American village is much uglier than an English village.

It did not occur to him that both these statements are perfectly true, perfectly compatible with each other and perfectly relevant to the truth I was concerned to prove. Journalistically speaking, one was The Attack on America and the other was The Defence of America —both excellent stunts, but needing to be taken up by two separate sentimentalists and not by one rationalist.

Of course, in so far as I was attacking or defending anything, it was not America at all. In the first case I was defending the normal life of man, and in the second the special landscape of England. In the first, I pointed out that Mencken and Lewis, being heathens and therefore pessimists, had really passed from deriding Main Street to deriding Man State, the city of Mansoul; the heart of man. Sceptics of that school have got down to asking, not whether there is good cultural tradition in a town full of chewing gum and chatter about dollars, but whether there is any good in a life that revolves around the baby and the wife and the working day. They are no longer merely mocking the provincial vices, but also the primeval virtues of the American village. To that question it is quite irrelevant that the American village is ugly.

In dealing with that question, I did not discuss whether it is ugly or not. But in the other case I had quite another logical aim. I was pointing out that touching the beauty of the country-side, England is (as Shakespeare said) a precious gem—not only in being beautiful, but in being rare. Untravelled people think their own grass and woods stretch to the ends of the earth; they do not know they are living in a garden in a wilderness. And I gave the example that America, though it produces superb architecture in cities, has nowhere in its vast expanse produced anything but ugliness in its villages. Both points were directly relevant to what I had to explain, and, indeed, had been specially asked to explain. But one was A. A. (Against America) and the other was F. A. (For America). How could this mystery be explained, except by a Double Life, or perhaps a Dual Personality? I therefore assure my American friend that I am not inconsistent, but on the contrary, strictly inconsistent, in saying that an English village looks more human than an American village, but that even an American village is more human than an art colony or a Communist settlement.

Among the last of these last words on America may well be this: that the Republic is anything except a Republic. I have remarked that it is in a sense a democracy, though mostly in that loose and inaccurate modern sense, by which we say democratic when we should say egalitarian. The average private person does have that sort of self-respect which is no respecter of persons; though it may be answered that this is easier in a political world where persons are not so respectable. This may be called democracy in the sense that the democracy does not look up to the demagogue. The mob rather looks down on its masters than looks up to them.

But in that ancient and majestic name of the Republic inherited from the very fundamentals of Rome, there is another idea present, and in the American Republic it is entirely absent. It is indeed a quaint paradox to suggest that there could be any meaning in the distinction between the names of two modern political parties. But in the case of Democrats and Republicans there is a difference in the names, even if there is no difference in the parties. And a man might be democratic, in the general sense of sympathizing with the mob rather than its masters, without being Republican at all.

The citizens of the United States are not Republican at all; least of all the Republicans. For that old-world title of The Public Thing, which was still used in the feudal Middle Ages as well as in the Roman Empire, had in it the idea that every man has a direct relation to the realm or commonweal, more direct than he has to any masters or patrons in private life; that whatever he does in bargaining with equals or in the relations of client or advocate, he should be conscious of the great background of the Forum and the Capitol.

Every State in the Union has a Capitol in that old classical style, and some of them in a very fine architectural style. But the one place where it is present to the eye is the one place where it has entirely vanished from the mind. The Capitol does not dominate the skyscrapers and the sky signs; it certainly does not intimidate the people who put up the sky signs. Americans are good neighbours rather than good citizens. That pure and positive public spirit has faded from their life more than from that of any people in the world.

What is the matter with America is that every American has been tacitly or loudly taught that his job is not only more vital than his vote, but more vital than that virtue of public spirit which the vote represents. But because of his private virtue, which is stronger than his

-{ 185 }-

public virtue, this has not produced mere selfishness. What it has produced is a queer sort of feudal loyalty. And, just as in the Dark Ages, the result of mere feudal loyalty has been mere feudal anarchy. The reporter whose only duty is to report for his paper, the salesman whose only duty is to call for his boss, have created an atmosphere like that of the half-barbarous heroism of the Song of Roland, in which a man must lose hair and hide for his lord.

Hence America is full of organizations, but not of organization; in the sense of order. It is utterly disorganized by its organizations. They all have a sort of feudal fidelity and ferocity; they are all, in that sense, like the criminal organizations. Nowhere do they so completely despise the State, nowhere do they so utterly disunite the State, as in what we call the United States. There is a danger that what Grant and Lincoln saved under the name of the Union may deserve the special name of the Disunion.

Things might have been different if the political successors of Grant and Lincoln had understood the State in the old simpler sense; or, in other words, if the Republicans had been Republicans. Unfortunately it was they, even more than their opponents, who encouraged this commercial scramble, as if it were part of the vigour and therefore the virtue of America. Consequently it is very difficult to get the individual wage earner to con-

sider seriously whether it is good for the nation that
newspapers should succeed in their stunts, that sales-
men should succeed in their sales, that advertisers should
advertise and boosters should boost. He feels in a very
human way that it is good for his salary; he feels in a
very proper way that it is good for his family; he feels
in a sort of feudal way that it is good for his firm. I
doubt whether he feels, or specially pretends to feel,
that it is good for his country.

Anyhow, it is very bad for his country. It is the
beginning of all the crime and corruption and over-
production and under-employment against which he
himself is beginning to react and rebel. And its causes lie
far back in the spiritual story of the people, in the religious rather than in the political history of America.
All this worldliness had a strange root in unworldliness.
It arose because the nation arose not with unity in philosophy, but with variety in fanaticism; with sects built on
special dogmas or on the denial of special dogmas; on
something that was not merely private judgment, but
also particular judgment.

It would be very difficult to draw the line, or to fix
the date, between the last officialism of the dying
Roman Empire and the first feudalism of the Dark Ages.
But we could say with confidence that by the sixth or
seventh centuries, organized society had passed its zenith
and was declining toward a lower state of culture. I

-{ 187 }-

think the zenith of Christian ideas was at the moment when men had got rid of slavery and were beginning to attempt small property—before small property had been swallowed up in large property. I think it was at the moment when men were already national but were still capable of being international.

I think the collapse into capitalism is very like the collapse into feudalism; and in that way is not unlike a collapse into barbarism. Men may come to like being herded and guarded by big firms, as they came to like being herded and guarded by big feudal lordships. But it is a fall, and in the special case of America, it is especially a fall of the Republic. But men still talked of the Roman Empire as the Republic, even when everything was in fact becoming feudal; and similarly the Republic is still often mentioned, even in capitalist America.

But in America these lesser loyalties, the duty of holding down the job, the duty of selling the goods, are more positive and less negative than they are in England. And this unnatural individualism, supported by many vigorous and manly virtues, is historically due to the old individualism in religion. In England it is rather the decline of the romance of the gentleman than the presence of the romance of the salesman. In America it is still the individual making good in trade, because it was originally the individual making good in goodness;

that is, in salvation of the soul. Their religion was not republican enough; it was not common enough for a Commonwealth. And so at last religion surrendered to the trick of trade; learned from hucksters and hustlers how to "put it over"; counted converts like customers; and thought rather of selling the goods than of seeking the good.

This is the only real tragedy of America, and I have enough respect for the old Puritan to lament it. It is more tragic than comic to hear Puritans still denouncing Papists for pageantry and mummery, and then advertising their own chapels with theatricals and coloured lights. What the Puritans would not do for the glory of God or the beauty of woman, what they would not tolerate in priests or pardon in poets, they have done as a mere surrender to window-dressing and the wind-bags of publicity. So the commercial scramble has reacted on a new problem. The problem of the great American democracy is in the conflict between the good and the bad principles I have indicated here; the great popular sense of worth and work, the unconscious heroism of the Average Man of Whitman, the old republican simplicity; and, on the other side, the tawdry and inadequate ideal of mere ambition and unrest.

Americans would be delightful if Americans would leave them alone. But there is an electric fan of hot air stirring them up endlessly to effort rather than effect.

-꒦ 189 ꒦-

Nevertheless, they have this great advantage over us: that their older sanity was solidified into a creed; but I think that creed must become more rather than less Christian. It is no case for the Pharisee; heaven knows the English have often forgotten the cross on their flag. But I think that the crossless flag may yet become a symbol of something; by whose stars we are illumined, and by whose stripes we are healed.

-: 190 :-

XIV. RETURN TO THE VISION

THE real case against Revolution is this; that there always seems to be so much more to be said against the old *regime* than in favour of the new *regime*. It is not so much that it is always a bad thing that things should burst; but that they so often burst in the wrong place. Thus the Bolshevist Revolution burst in the wrong place in the towns. These were so rare and unrelated to the rest of Russia, that it was almost as if a revolution in our big towns had begun in the lunatic asylums. The result was that there arose something so horribly inhuman and unnatural that it did really deserve to be called the Dictatorship of the Proletariat. In other words, it consisted of men who became tyrants while they were still slaves . . . yes, even in the Socialist sense of wage-slaves. The slavery peculiar to the town became the tyranny covering the country-side. And in the country-side, the men who had once been serfs and had become peasants, owning their own land, were forced to become slaves owning no land; because that is the law of the towns. All that would have been better, if the main explosion had come in the main bulk of the nation; if the Russian Revolution had been like the French Revolution. Much is said today against Rousseau and the romantic revolutionaries who idealized life on the land. But it is better to be romantic about a real thing like the land than to be realistic about an unreal thing like the Economic Theory of History. In an evil hour, Russia fell under the power, not of a French philosopher, but of a German Jewish economist. Karl Marx was the very opposite of a lover of the land. He was a typical townsman, as are most Jewish intellectuals of his type, and he could not understand peasants any more than the present Russian Government can. But the trouble burst in the wrong place; it burst in the town and permitted bookish people to enslave it by a book. Karl Marx became the Koran of all those half-Oriental tribes; with something of the Moslem reverence for anything written on a piece of paper. For Marxians, like all materials, are of necessity mystics. For Matter is an unknown God; whereas Spirit was made flesh and dwelt among us.

That is only one example; a hundred others could be given; of the way in which the cause of Revolution is so often right and the result of Revolution so often wrong. But the case can be put more favourably to the Revolutionary idea; and the point of the case is really this. There is a sense in which we may truly say that the fault of many revolutions was in not being revolutionary enough. I mean that the evil did not come through what they destroyed; but rather through what they retained. Certainly the combination of the two

-{ 192 }-

almost always left a false and unfortunate heritage. An
Englishman writing for an American paper may most
naturally take the example of the American Revolution.
I am far from certain how many Americans or Englishmen would agree with me. I sometimes have a dark
suspicion that I should have to defend the American
Revolution more often against Americans than against
Englishmen. But, in any case, my own personal view of
it is this. I will not say that Americans were right to
overthrow the power of King George; for in fact there
was no power of King George to overthrow. England
was not a monarchy. England was already an aristocracy. But Americans, in my judgment, were perfectly
entitled to break away from that aristocracy. An aristocracy is a system which has its advantages and disadvantages; but for those who really wish to live the
democratic life even the advantages were disadvantages.
And, when all is discounted from the mere cant of
emancipation, it is true that a poor man leaving the
English country-side for the American coast did become
a free man; even if he was starved or frozen in a blizzard
or eaten by a grizzly bear. He had no longer a master or
a lord. At home the advantage of aristocracy was having
a good squire; the disadvantage was having a bad squire.
Some may even prefer a bad squire to a bear. But it is
true, as far as it goes, that in breaking with aristocracy,
the revolted colonies did open a democracy for those

who care to be democrats. It was not the English things they ruined which ruined them. It was the English things they retained.

All the troubles of the Revolution came from being Conservatives. For instance, they were so persistently and pig-headedly Conservative that they preserved Puritanism. There was really no reason why that entirely local English or Scottish prejudice should have pursued them across the free Atlantic into the wide prairies of the land of promise. The Puritans who sailed in the *Mayflower* were altogether too respectful to the England of Elizabeth and Charles the First. They should have thrown their Plymouth religion into the sea somewhere; and started clean as Pagans, since it was impossible for them to start as Christians. The great Jefferson did indeed largely realize this; and made the philosophy of the Republic out of that normal and universal Deism which really is natural to most men, when they are neither Puritans, atheists nor Catholics. But I will firmly maintain, though I fear I shall not carry all my readers with me, that the Puritanism which was brought from Plymouth has produced, and is still producing, a crop of corruptions and difficulties which were really no part of the natural American situation at all. The destroyers of tea in Boston Harbour did not destroy sufficiently. The subscribers to the Declaration of Independence were not independent enough. Given the impossible position in England, between Puritanism and aristocracy, it would have been better if they had drifted even further away. It would have been better if the New World had been something more like a New Creation.

I do not deal here directly with religion in the sense of religious proof, and its supreme claims; many are aware what particular creed would condition all my remarks on that side; as a Catholic I know well of what sacred thing the Puritans carried the fragments, and should always treat it and them with due regard. But, speaking of this single matter of simplifying American politics, and considering history apart from theology, so far as it can be considered, I repeat that it would be easier to reach a religious and political understanding today, if the Pilgrims had not been Puritans, and had not carried their sects and sectarian battles to the New World. Nay, in that sense it would be better if the natural religion of Americans had been like that of American Indians. They had better have lifted hands together to the Great Spirit walking above woods and clouds; a very natural religion; not unlike Jefferson's. For the Red God is at least a god of the beginnings; like the Red Clay of Adam; indeed we may say that, in the Bible, the First Man was a Red Man. Such a natural religion of origins might have eventually brought men nearer to ancient truths; even to the ancient truths of Christianity. And for my own faith (if it were here in question) Jesuits sometimes find it easier to convert Red Indians than Black Protestants.

It is true, of course, that at one time Puritanism was itself a Revolution. But it was a very remote Revolution; for all of us very remote in time and for Americans very remote in place. It was a curious crack in one corner of Europe, three hundred years ago, when all Europe was broken up by the upheaval of many other things, and many very contrary things, by the Paganism of the Renaissance, by the new pride of the Princes, by the greed and luxury of the New Rich. In any case, neither its virtues nor its vices are in the faintest degree sympathetic to the general spirit of the world today. It is a ruin, but a colossal ruin; and a ruin which is scattered over whole countries, and even whole continents, like the giant limbs of Ammon in the poem. And with that fact we come to another of the general considerations that must be taken into account in estimating the advantages and disadvantages of the revolutionary tradition. For everything is a tradition; even a Revolution.

It is a true point in the case against Revolution, that the world is so often cluttered up with the cold remains of old revolutions. What really stands in the way of the new novelty is the old novelty; which sometimes still considers itself new. For, after all, there are few institutions, however ancestral and antiquated, which do not

work back to some sort of revolution. Not only American democracy, but also English aristocracy was created,
in that sense, by revolution. What was called the Glorious Revolution of 1688 finally and firmly established
that system of great squires from which the later emigrants escaped to find freedom in America. But I admit
that it is a rather needless degradation of the word "Revolution" to apply it to the affair of 1688. The Glorious
Revolution was not a revolution, even if it was a rebellion. As a matter of fact, it was a plot. It was the
work of a few cold-blooded courtiers and conspiring
nobles, betraying James the Second by a palace revolution in which the people had no part. The American
Revolution was a real revolution, in whatever way the
people were divided; in so far as its leaders appealed to a
sort of abstract and primeval truth; like the makers of a
new world. But even here, in the matter of the mere
politicians of 1688, we may find the same point that I
noted touching Puritanism. The American Republic
really inherited rather too much than too little of the old
party politics of England. We might say that the West
has suffered only too much from the Westminster Election; just as it has suffered only too much from the
Westminster Confession. The Party Man as well as the
Puritan ought to have been drowned in crossing the
Atlantic. Indeed I have more personal sympathy with
those innocent and perhaps crazy enthusiasts who

thought they were leaving all worldly pomps and fictions behind them when they set foot on the virgin land of the free. I sympathize more with the honest gentleman who threw his wig into the sea, before sailing into Boston Harbour. The act really amounted to a parable and even to a pun. He threw away the wig; it would have been better to have thrown away the Whig.

Nay, there is another injustice to America even in the common talk about Americanization. In the mere worship of machinery, in the mere worship of money, in the headlong materialism that invents and exploits and sells with blind optimism, it is true that America on the whole advanced further; but it is not true that America advanced first. It seems to me only common fairness for an Englishman to admit that it was England that originally involved the world in this doubtful and dangerous departure from the traditions of Europe. To take the obvious example; the Steam Engine is as English as Shakespeare; though Puffing Billy has not remained such an inspiration as Poetic Will. I am not at all sure that, to a man of the time of Cobbett, for instance, England did not stand relatively for the town and America for the country-side. Much of the talk of emigrants, at that period, was rather of the sort that celebrates the West as what was afterwards called the Wild West. Heaven forbid that I should suggest that there is now anything resembling the Tame West; but in England there is less and less talk of anything beyond the West End. The urban limitation has closed upon us even more narrowly than upon the new cities and what we call the West End has something of the character of the End of the World. Now the whole point of the old vision of America was that there was no End of the World. It was a reckless and romantic vision, of course, and many died of it in deserts and deep canyons; but that was the vision, and it is not always understood, especially since conditions have altered and limited even America like a walled town. It is a real difficulty for historians that the strong motives of one generation are the stale jests of the next. A hundred American humorists, to say nothing of Mr. P. G. Wodehouse, have taught us to intone in a derisive chorus the famous phrase about "the great open spaces, where men are men." But there is something in it, for all that; if we only express it by saying that life in a modern town, whatever else it is is not Normalcy. The Wild and Woolly aphorism is true; in the sense that if men are to be men, they will require rather more open spaces. Their real, original sociological object in going to America was to find those open spaces. It was *not* to find more engineers and electric batteries and mechanical gadgets in the home. These may have been the results of America; they were not the causes of America. So that here again, even in the case of the admittedly American energy in industrial machinery, I may be permitted the paradox of a doubt. I rather doubt whether America was founded to do these things. I rather incline to believe that America was founded to escape from these things. I darkly suspect that England was already beginning to be crushed between colliding cities, caught up in roaring and rending wheels, feeling the threat of the throttling industrialism that has since overpowered her, that men from England and Scotland and Ireland and Western Europe began to think of the unfathomable vistas of the new sunset lands. Therefore, while I should heartily support an Englishman resisting the Americanization of England, I am not quite sure whether what he resists was not originally the Anglicizing of America.

I write these words, therefore, in some sense to ease my national conscience. I am only too well accustomed to politicians and diplomatists, presuming to speak for England, who pay heavy and greasy compliments to the Fathers of the American Republic and the fighters in the American Revolution; who say exactly the right thing about George Washington, subject to a hazy idea that he was identical with Abraham Lincoln. It has always seemed to me that such men were only insulted by such praise. The men who made the Revolution in America are now mocked even in America, let alone England or Europe. But I for one feel it due to those great men to say that all subsequent trouble has not come from the things that they began, but from the things that they borrowed. It was not the conception of life outlined in the Declaration of Independence that was wrong; it was the thousand things that have come in since to perplex it; and many of them have come from England and from Europe. The great Revolution failed to attain those high levels of equality and luminous justice to which its first promise had pointed; not because Americans were wrong to resist a German called George the Third, but because they continued to revere a Frenchman called Calvin, a Scotchman called Macaulay, an Englishman called Herbert Spencer, and all the rest of the dreary Whig and Puritan and industrial rationalism of what we call in England the Victorian Age. In this matter I am on the side of the old idealistic democrats. The vision was all right; it is the revision that is all wrong. America, instead of being the open agricultural commonwealth for which its founders hoped, has become the dumping-ground of all the most dismal ideas of decaying epochs in Europe, from Calvinism to industrialism. Even the American features which most offend a European, the extravagant exaggeration of commercial competition, or mechanical invention, or journalistic violence, are not ideas of the Revolution. They are ideas that have immigrated into America after the Revolution. For my part, I wish that Jefferson's democracy had remained immune from them. I wish it had cared as little for George Stephenson as for George the Third. I wish it had been as remote from Lord North-cliffe as from Lord North.

PART III

OTHER ESSAYS

I. THE SPIRIT OF THE AGE IN LITERATURE

THE Spirit of the Age is not a Spirit; it is not really spiritual, for by definition it is not immortal. If the phrase in relation to literature is already almost traditional, it is a series of monuments of mortality. Hazlitt used it, I think, to summarize his sketches; and it is amusing to reflect how different has been the age on which we look back from that to which Hazlitt looked forward. He was as far out in the change he hoped for as in the things he thought unchangeable; it would have surprised him, for instance, to learn that he could not take one of his country walks, and give himself up to thinking, without being killed by about six successive motor-cars. Matthew Arnold, writing round about 1870, used a similar phrase but carefully translated it into German. It is again amusing to think that if he had lived till 1914, he would have hurriedly translated it back into English. By which I do not mean that he was either a snob or a turncoat, but that he believed in The Spirit of the Age and suffered accordingly. And it is obvious that what is roughly and rather inaccurately called the Post-War world has a new atmosphere of its own, not only different from all that Hazlitt or Arnold knew, but very different from all that Hazlitt or Arnold expected.

This atmosphere in all the arts, and notably in literature, is easily discernible, though not perhaps easily definable. If we were forced to fix on a single word, perhaps the word Syncopation would best express the artistic element; for syncope, which in medicine is a malady, in æsthetics is a movement. To put it less pedantically, the world has shown a disposition to come out in spots, even if we admit that some of them are beauty spots. A quality which literary reviewers suddenly start calling sporadic, but which those who love the noble English language will prefer to call patchy, appeared simultaneously in all the arts; music cut up into notes, pictures cut up into cubes, prose cut up into impressions and episodes, and poetry often cut up into isolated images. There went with this a love, not only of vivid or violent colour, but of very jagged outline or pattern; as if to emphasize the fact of something broken off sharply from everything else. In the case of literature, the thing so broken off was the individual mind, or even a subdivision of the individual mind. It has been said that Protestantism isolated the soul; however this may be, it is true that this kind of modernism isolates not only the mind but the mood. It not only cuts up mankind into men, but it actually cuts up a man into moods. That is the fairest way of judging much that is severely

judged in the irresponsibility and anarchy of some sex
novels by novelists not personally ignoble. Quite apart
from morality, the old love story had a natural artistic
unity, for it had a single end, apart from a happy ending.
But the story not of love but of loves, under existing
conditions, is bound to be a string of episodes without
much effect on each other, for that is how the man of
that school regards them. It may be very wrong to
hunt a boar or a stag, but you could make a hunting-
song of it, or a story with a climax when the wild boar
turned to bay. But if your philosophy is hardly even
that of a naturalist catching butterflies, but almost that
of an idler or idiot catching flies, you cannot make a
climax, but only a series. One effect of this isolation is a
certain irresponsibility about communal ideals, which
can be best exemplified in poetry; since it contrasts so
sharply with the old world of William Morris or Walt
Whitman. The change is in the loss of positive ideals.
Whitman was an enthusiast for Democracy; his country-
man, Mr. Mencken, to put it mildly, is not an enthusiast
for Democracy; but neither is he an enthusiast for anything opposed to Democracy. Morris's Earthly Paradise
does not exist on earth, but Mr. Aldous Huxley will
believe in a heavenly paradise long before he believes
in an earthly one.

When Swinburne called his work Songs Before Sunrise, and posed as a prophet wrapped in a mantle watch-

ing the red daybreak of revolution, he was almost
exactly like the man in Mark Twain who came out
hurriedly, bundled in a blanket, to watch the sun rise
on the Alps, and after watching the orb anxiously for
some time, found he was just in time to see it set. Swinburne's republicanism was red enough in colour, if
rather cloudy in form, but it was certainly the red of
sunset and the reverse of the red of dawn. The epoch
which he supposed to be beginning was in fact at that
very moment ending, and we could hardly do better
in dating the present literary epoch than to date it from
that sad Swinburnian end. To take a metaphor even
more Swinburnian than that of sunrise: he was the last
foaming wave, sometimes (it might be hinted) a rather
frothy wave, which made the high-water mark of that
great flood-tide, which in politics we call the French
Revolution, and in poetry measure by the names of
Shelley and Landor and Beranger and Victor Hugo;
with some previous movements in Burns or Blake.
Roughly speaking, Shelley was at the beginning of the
period and Swinburne at the end of it, and between them
was all that counted of the movement which identified
poets with prophets of revolt, which set the laurel crown
of the bard directly against the golden crown of all other
kings, and conceived the lyre as chiefly strung to sound
the praises of Liberty. That conception is dead. It died,
not so much when Swinburne died, but rather when

Swinburne wrote his first Imperial sonnet in praise of the South African War.

It is rather odd to remark, in passing, and rather salutary for professional revolutionists and pioneers, that there is almost always a sort of break, of boredom or disgust, immediately after some very flamboyant figure has defied the convention, and therefore become the fashion. The Bohemian, who is seen everywhere in Society, boldly despising Society, has a high old time while it lasts, and really makes the best of both worlds, the wilderness and the drawing-room, but it does not last very long. Very early in the nineteenth century, it was already old-fashioned to enjoy Byron; as it will never be old-fashioned to enjoy Chaucer or Homer. The ringlets and whiskers of his darkling heroes and heroines soon began to have a particular sort of staleness, which does not apply to monkish tonsures or ancient Argive beards. It is the staleness of old fashion-plates, which is never felt in old pictures. The Byronic spirit became old-fashioned because it had been the fashion; but, above all, because it had been the very latest, loudest, most daring and revolutionary fashion. When somebody or something has reached that wild, supreme ecstasy of novelty, it is suddenly stricken old, and stamped for ever with its date and death. Nobody can carry it any further; nobody wants to do it again; nobody even wants to do it better. It has been too much of a success, and something of a secret and subtle vulgarity, that lies in the very heart of success, has become flagrant in it and sent forth a savour of shame. And by this I mean a general truth about human life, not a petty sneer at the personal life of Byron, whom I admire as a poet and even sympathize with as a man, much more than it is now the fashion to do. But it is true that because Byron was a man full of the Spirit of the Age, his very portrait seemed rapidly to grow aged; like the portrait of Dorian Gray. And similarly, it was because Swinburne was so very certain that he was a revolutionary poet, that there is a reaction against him even as a poet, and an utter oblivion of him as a revolutionary. This does not prove that it is wrong to be a revolutionary; on the contrary, many of the things against which Byron and Swinburne revolted were in fact very revolting. But it does mean that this sort of innovation and insurrection is likely to be as much disliked immediately after its triumph as immediately before. The rebel may be right to make a rebellion, but he will not make a dynasty. The man most brilliant and conspicuous with the Spirit of the Age will have an air of horrible and offensive familiarity to the people of the next age. I will not apply the parable in any personal fashion, but it is well to realize that if, there be anywhere at this moment a man who seems vivid and vibrant with the new forces in literature, picked out by the spotlight in the perfect jazz pattern, and moving in faultless triumph to the vital and essential jazz tune, we may be sure it is that man, and no milder specimen, who will seem in forty years as faded as a rhetorical ode to Julia or Matilda, or the Byronic verses in an old album about a rose and a tear.

Let us realize to start with, therefore, that in so far as The Spirit of the Age is only the Spirit of the Age and is not also The Spirit of the Ages, and of all that is before and after the ages, it is a spirit that very quickly evaporates, and perhaps most quickly where it has seemed particularly pungent and strong. Byron and Swinburne did, in their day, emphatically go to our heads; but, to judge by current criticism, they have left many with little more than headaches. This is most notable in the criticism of poetry; but it is still more notable that so much of the poetry is criticism. We need not discuss fully the justice or injustice of the charges of mere ugliness and unworthiness made against recent verse. But nobody will deny the general sense in which Swinburne, if not one of the most perfect of poets, was at least one of the most poetical of poets. And no one will deny that, in comparison at least, he has been followed very abruptly by a race of prosaic poets. Much of it is merely negative and destructive; the sort of analysis that has generally been presented in prose. Swinburne was accused of sacrificing sense to sound, or of writing mere nonsense for the sake of melody. Some of the new poets write what a coarse, careless world might mistake for nonsense; but they never bribe or insult us with anything that we could mistake for melody. I confess I think the charge against Swinburne was sometimes just; that having said, "With life before and after," which might mean something, though the opposite of what Swinburne meant, he went on cheerfully to add, "And death beneath and above," which means nothing at all. I admit that merely to provide a rhyme for the beautiful line "Blossom by blossom, the spring begins," he did not scruple to write of "the season of snows and sins," as if the most respectable people were always wicked in winter. But I think it will also be admitted, on the other side, that a recent poet who announced his intentions in the lines:

> And I shall sing
> By the blood in stone images.

also indicates a purpose that is not entirely clear; and that on the other hand, when it comes to singing, stone images do not sing quite so successfully as Swinburne.

This, however, is merely a superficial view of the contrast; and by itself would make the critic figure far too much as a *laudator temporis acti*. I am in no way tied to defend the nonsense of the Swinburne period, any more than the nonsense of the Ezra Pound period, but I am quite ready to recognize the sense in both, and especially the sense in which the two senses are separate. I began this sketch with the name of Swinburne, because, while it is the latest and nearest of the great names of the nineteenth century, it also marks the very sharp change to the new atmosphere of the twentieth. And the first change to notice is that which I did in fact notice first; when I spoke of the red daybreak of the revolutionary dreams. One of the things which has suddenly, silently, and curiously, completely collapsed, is the notion of an enthusiasm which was poetical and also political. I say an enthusiasm; for the new analytic writers might well be capable of writing political satire. That is, verse which expresses, not our enthusiasm for politics, but our lack of enthusiasm for politicians. It is true that the latest satire is sometimes a little obscure, and that the heartening energy with which the poets hold up a politician to public ridicule and contempt is sometimes a little weakened by the public having a difficulty in grasping what they are talking about, or understanding a word they say. But on that side their work might still be forcible; and need be none the less so for being as involved as Browning or Donne. But the positive, and especially the popular or collective, side of sociology seems to have suddenly become impossible in poetry. Poetry has become more than normally individualistic. The individualist can write a song; but not a song with a chorus.

Such a change in poetry necessarily has causes that are political rather than poetical. I shall therefore say the less about them; especially as the inquiry would involve the explanation of views of my own, which are here irrelevant and seem to some eccentric. My own opinion is that the younger generation, especially the most intelligent among them, are conscious of the coming of a new social system, which they do not either love or desire, but which they do not hate sufficiently to destroy. The idea that Republics would make the world perfect was soon destroyed—by the Republics. The idea that Socialism would make the world perfect has been left in a more kindly haze; because Socialism has been abandoned by the Socialists. But meanwhile the old private property and liberty were being absorbed or destroyed, not by the Socialists, but by the Capitalists. They are being destroyed by the Trusts; by the sort of Business Government now everywhere prevailing. Now poets cannot be expected to sing wild happy lyrics in praise of Business Government. At the same time, poets, especially modern poets, cannot be expected to die on the barricades, in a revolution against Business Government. It is to some extent to the interest of poets that people should be business-like—even in the publishing business. So long as the Trust State is fairly humane and works steadily, there is nothing to fight about; but there is precious little to sing about. For Business Government has neither authority nor liberty. Whether or no this explanation be right, it is certainly a paradox that this patchy isolation of the mind should exist under social conditions of almost inhuman sameness and centralization. But the paradox is in any case a very practical part of the tragedy. Wilde, in The Soul of Man Under Socialism, unconsciously uttered a very profound warning—against Socialism. It was the warning that even under Socialism the soul might have a tragedy like that of Wilde. Under the Servile State the soul will be yet more horribly free. There will be nothing to prevent a man losing his soul, as long as he does not lose his time or his ticket or his place in the bread queue. We need not be surprised, therefore, if the laborious organization and combination of our time encircles a singular loneliness. It is more important to note that the new literature has some of the merits of loneliness; an increasing refusal to be encouraged by newspaper clap-trap or made cheerful to order, a certain disgust with Party Systems, and not a little open-mindedness to the ideas of the past as well as the ideas of the future; at least, in the finest minds, a refusal to be tied to the ideas of the present. As usual, the wisest men of the age are not dominated by the spirit of the age. But perhaps the best summary in the matter of our own age would be this; that the stupid people are sneering at the last generation and the intelligent people are sneering at their

own generation. But I think it must be admitted that
most of them are sneering.

This unsociable quality in the intellect, which can
co-exist with so much superficial sociability or herding
in the habits, is the most outstanding fact about really
able writers in recent days. One of its manifestations is
a verbal eccentricity in works of a talent that goes beyond the eccentric. It is something like the secret language that is invented by a child. *Ulysses* contains a
number of very queer words; though perhaps none
queerer than *Ulysses*. For the comparison is curious in
itself, seeing that throughout a prolonged pagan epic
Homer manages to be very pure in very plain language,
while Joyce manages to be very coarse in very esoteric
language. There are whole passages, of the sort on which
the moral argument turns, which are dark to the point
of decency. He has been compared to Rabelais, but the
very comparison should be enough to show us vividly
the difference made by The Spirit of the Age. It is the
whole force of Rabelais that he seems to roar like ten
thousand men; that one of his giants is like a multitude
turned into a man. What he roars may not always be
very distinct or intelligible, any more than the roar of
an actual rabble or mob; but we know that what is being
shouted is something quite normal and human, even if
it be what some would call bestial. But we do not feel, or
at least I do not feel, that James Joyce ever speaks for

anybody except James Joyce. We may call this individuality or insanity or genius or what we will; but it belongs to its time because of this air of having invented its own language; and moved a little further away from anything like a universal language. The new Ulysses is the opposite of the old Ulysses, for the latter moved amid ogres and witches with a level-headed and almost prosaic common sense, while the former moves among common lamp-posts and public-houses with a fixed attitude of mind more fantastic than all the fairy-tales. I am not here either adequately praising or adequately criticizing this much controverted work; I am merely using it as an illustration of the isolation of one mind, or even of one mood. Rabelais sometimes seems confusing, because he is like twenty men talking at once; but Joyce is rather inaudible, because he is talking to himself.

The late D. H. Lawrence is generally quoted, along with such a writer as James Joyce, as a typical product of the time. Personally I suspect that there was rather more in Lawrence than any mere spirit of any mere age, especially such an age. Whether what was inside him ever really came out of him, or ever came out except tail foremost, in the wrong order and the wrong proportion, may be more doubtful. I fancy that most of his faults could be referred to the one not unpardonable fault of impatience. His time and training made it inevitable that he should grope. But his temper made it natural that he should not so much grope as grab. Like so many men of his type, he started cocksure that he was right, and gradually grew more and more fruitful and human as he discovered that he was wrong. He would never, naturally enough, have put it in the form that he was wrong; and indeed it would be truer to say that he found himself capable of being much more right. But anyhow, he, much more than any of his comrades and contemporaries, had something of that old religious spirit of the revolutionist; the constructive revolutionist who makes himself responsible for a new world. He did, if in the groping modern fashion, try to get to grips with our ultimate relations with God and woman and nature, and the things on which a new world can be built. He had much more of the childlike and honourable seriousness of men like Morris and Thoreau and Walt Whitman. He did not always sneer. But the moral chaos of his time delayed the self-education of his genius, and it marks the same spirit of syncopation or separatism that it had to be merely self-education. He lived in an age crowded with schools and schooling, and all the things he naturally hated; but there was no education because there was no tradition. There was no communal inheritance of virtues or right relations, and therefore his virtues, like all the virtues of his generation, had to be individual and rather irritable.

Something of the same abnormal reaction towards the normal may be observed in the ripening of the remarkable talent of Miss Rebecca West, who has of late tended more and more to reconstruct for herself the tradition that her friends have destroyed for her. Her friends and intellectual interests, also, have been more among the survivals of the old visionaries of social construction; the old guard of the systematizers of whom perhaps the last and greatest remains in Mr. Bernard Shaw. We must look elsewhere for a new and clean-cut case of the more modern attitude, and on the whole, perhaps, the last philosophic phase is best expressed in one of the most brilliant of living writers: Mr. Aldous Huxley. He would not even be complimented to be compared to Shelley, and nobody is likely to make the comparison. But he would not even be complimented to be compared to Shaw, in so far as Shaw stands for that stock of nineteenth-century ideals of simplification and perfectibility, which, along with his vegetarianism, Shaw really inherits from Shelley. Mr. Aldous Huxley not only does not inherit or continue those ideals which broadly begin with Rousseau, he turns on them and rends them. He is a very rare specimen, a real realist; in the sense that he is a realist at the expense of new things as well as old, and ready to testify against revolt as well as against tyranny. In truth he is ready to testify against anything; it would be rather more difficult to say what he is testifying to or for. Perhaps the change I describe, from the revolt of the nineteenth century to the realism of the twentieth, could not be better measured than by the distance between two dates; the day on which Mr. H. G. Wells, laying the foundations of the first of his Utopias, declared that its first principle should be that Original Sin is a lie—to the day when Mr. Aldous Huxley, heir of the great scientific house in its next generation, wrote that the mediæval mind was far wiser than the nineteenth-century minds, because it recognized Original Sin. There is no doubt at all about Mr. Aldous Huxley recognizing Original Sin. There are moments when he seems to drift darkly towards that Calvinist exaggeration that was called Total Depravity. Indeed, while I always admire and often agree with his suggestions, there does seem to be also a darker suggestion, unconscious but none the less uncanny, of that sort of Manichæan mysticism which traced the roots of evil in nature itself; a strange wilderness of vision, without form or frontier, in which everything is repulsive because nothing is forbidden. This, being but a guess at the subconscious, is perhaps unfair; it is fairer to say that there returns with Aldous Huxley something of the spirit of Jonathan Swift; the rocky sincerity, the splendid scorn of snobbery, especially intellectual snobbery, the virile impatience with unworthy praise; but, with the rest, something of that strange self-torturing itch of the sensitive man to insist on ugliness because of his love of beauty. In Huxley, as in Swift, the passages called unpleasant are really unpleasant; perhaps they would be worse if they were pleasant. They can hardly be called sensual, for they do not even please the senses. I may well end this rude outline with the name of this remarkable writer, because he does exactly mark the way in which the mind of man has come full circle since the middle of the nineteenth century. He is the low-water mark, as I have said that Swinburne was the high-water mark, of that foaming or frothing sea of humanitarian hope. Yet there was a truth behind the impatient discovery of the Millennium, as well as behind the belated rediscovery of the Fall. Nor will man be permanently satisfied with the pessimism of Huxley, any more than with the optimism of Whitman. For man knows there is that within him that can never be valued too highly, as well as that within him which can never be hated too much; and only a philosophy which emphasizes both, violently and simultaneously, can restore the balance to the brain.

II. THE MIDDLEMAN IN POETRY

A RELATIVE and reasonable degree of sympathy between the world and its works of art is more and more rapidly disappearing today. The distance is increased with every advance of what are called the advanced schools of art. Even if we think the advance is really a progress, it is none the less certainly a progress that leaves the people behind. When a new experiment is made in poetry, one critic will say the poems are truly imaginative, another critic will say the poems are merely impudent; but neither will say that the poems are likely to be popular. Neither will say that if a blind man with a dog will go about singing them in Surbiton and Streatham, it is at all probable that ten suburbs will contend for the honour of being his birthplace. And that is the primary point that concerns me here; the widening breach between art and general appreciation. I will not discuss whether it is because the public has grown too stupid or the artists have grown too clever. I merely note that even those who advocate the wildest adventures in art no longer expect the people to keep pace with their adventures. I know there is a theory by which those who hail what is most new in the experiment declare that there is nothing new in the situation. They talk as if the

Elgin marbles had evoked howls of horror in the days of Phidias, and been understood at last by the time of Lord Elgin. They say that each masterpiece is a monstrosity until men grow used to it and call it a classic. But they are wrong. They are wrong in missing the whole proportion and therefore the whole point. There have always been disputes about art; but they have been disputes among normal people about matters of degree. There were any number of people who disliked Benvenuto Cellini; there were any number of people who probably preferred the clumsy and pretentious statues of Bandinelli. But there was not a whole crowd of men standing gaping and goggling in front of a statue of Cellini, wondering what in the world it was meant for, and how anybody could have the impudence to suppose that such a thing was a sculpture at all. In other words, there was not such a crowd as may have stood any day in Hyde Park in front of Mr. Epstein's memorial to Hudson. I repeat that I am not raising the question of whether Mr. Epstein or his critics are right in the quarrel; I am only pointing out that the quarrel between Cellini and his critics was a totally different sort of quarrel. I admit that it may mean that Mr. Epstein is more profound and original. I will even hint that it might mean that the Florentines four hundred years ago were more intelligent. But anyhow this new breach does exist; not about whether something is a good or bad statue or a good or bad poem; but simply about whether it is a statue at all or a poem at all. And *that* is what has created the new metaphysical middleman: the Interpreter between the artist and the world.

But now we pass to the second act of the tragedy. It presents the tragic irony of the interpreter who does not interpret. As a matter of fact the merchandise in question stops with the middleman and never gets any further. The friend, the favourable critic, the sympathizer with the new poetry, does not really popularize the poetry. He only creates a club or clique of sympathizers like himself, in which the poet is praised for his incapacity to become popular. Now although the sympathizers have little effect upon the public, they have a very definite effect upon the poet. The existence of the middleman has a certain special effect on the maker, even if it has no great effect on the general customer or consumer. The effect might perhaps be stated thus; that the middleman is always ready to receive raw material. He does not insist on having a finished product, pointed towards a certain immediate use of popularity, as did the much abused bookseller or the crowd listening to a minstrel. The very virtues of the interpreter make him tolerant of a broken or stammering speech to be interpreted. He is naturally a little proud of understanding what nobody else can understand, and therefore he does not really encourage the original speaker to make himself understood. The stammerer might really become a speaker, by straightforward practice in speaking to a crowd. The stammerer will always be a stammerer, so long as the stammer itself is regarded as an eccentricity of genius in the conversation of a clique. I am nowhere talking here of cowards or corrupt adventurers who would in any case fear to deliver their conception to the crowd; I am talking of those whose conception is as yet only conceived and not truly born into the world. The trouble with the interpreter is that he is too intelligent. He understands what the artist wants to say and even saves him the trouble of saying it—or at least of saying it in as pointed and polished a way as it could be said. As I say, he is willing to accept from the poet the raw material of a poem. He is delighted to accept hints for an unwritten poem; a poem that really remains un-written. He finds the poet "suggestive"; but he does not suggest that he should write the poem. He is content to know the poet has something in him; and does not really help to get it out of him.

It may seem harsh to say that a critic has too much sympathy. It may seem mad to say that he has too much understanding. But I do think that such understanding sometimes actually obstructs work that might be under-standed of the people The point is itself easily mis-understood. I am throwing out here something too tentative to be called a theory, and it may perhaps be approximately adumbrated in an example. Let us suppose that somebody has introduced us to the work of a new poet, of the sort that seems too often (to many people) to forget to be poetical in the effort to be new. Suppose he writes a more or less symbolic and perhaps obscure poem, about some demigod or demon or dominant being or other, and describes him in terms so arresting as to seem to some a little amusing. Suppose, let us say, that one line of the lyric runs, "He had trenches upon his face." The first effect of that line on a healthy mind is simply that it is funny. And as it is meant to be serious, it is a fault that it is funny. This is the first and the simplest but also one of the soundest of all critical tests. All poetry is like oratory, in so far as the pathetic orator implies the opening, "If you have tears, prepare to shed them now," and if a shout of laughter instantly goes up from the crowd, no critical arguments afterwards can prevent it from being a bad speech; and the same is really true of a bad song. The imaginary line I have suggested could only be a part of a song, if it were a comic song. It bears a pleasing resemblance to a refrain sung in happier days by Mr. Gus Elen, "And his face was like a map of Clapham Junction." That is indeed literature of a high order; but it belongs to gargoyles and the grotesque. He who shall assure us it has a classic and epic quality will leave us hesitating and even cold. And yet there may be something in it. It may be that you and I (being persons of almost inspired sublety and penetration) can see something of what the poet is really driving at, and are ourselves eager to explain it. We may say in effect: "Yes, yes; that is all very well, but you miss the point. What he wanted to say was hard anyhow; and he has said it somehow. He has seized on the word 'trenches'; and 'trenches' is exactly the right word. It may appear abrupt, but he has got the sense of *size,* in the face on which the very cuts were deep as dykes. He wants to describe something huge and catastrophic; something scarred on the grand scale; as the world was wounded by the world-war. The world's wounds were really and truly trenches. It would be inadequate to say cracks or chasms or fissures; they do not suggest something ploughed deep almost according to a colossal plan of ruin. There might be cracks in a walnut or fissure in a shell; it is just this strange word 'trench' which, when once you understand it, is awful and even appalling." I say this to you and you say it to me, and we proceed to form, if not a mutual admiration society, at least a society founded on a common admiration. Unfortunately, it is not in the full sense a common admiration. It is common to us, but not common to the common-wealth. The common people do not hear us gladly, except in the sense of uttering those cries of gladness that greeted Mr. Gus Elen. The commons do not

regard the poem as a common heritage, or the sort of
goods to be held in common. They continue to laugh
at the picture and the poet; but meanwhile the poet
has realized that we at least appreciate the picture. We
protect the poet from the public. We also keep the
public from the poet. We do harm.

For it seems to me that, if the poet were left to himself, and not prematurely flattered by a few prigs, who
happen to comprehend him before he is quite compre-
hensible, he might have worked in a harder and humbler
fashion, until he had made his whole image really com-
prehensible and complete. If he had been dealing, as
the old poets did, merely with a dull bookseller and the
common talk of the town, he might have tried a great
deal more strenuously to get the whole of his meaning
out into the broad daylight and moulded into the im-
agery of man. He might even have made it more indirect in form, but more direct in effect. He might have
cast about for some other way of saving the essential
but dangerous word "trench"; he might have wondered
vaguely if a verb would move more naturally than a
noun: and he might at last (who knows?) have evolved
some such experiment at this:

> . . . . but his brow
> Deep scars of thunder had intrenched, and care
> Sat on his faded cheek.

It may be retorted that this also will not be popular poetry. But it will be a great deal more popular than the sort that can only be a popular joke. Nobody will laugh, and many more people will learn. And they will learn not least from the bold and significant word "trench," which the poet has still used, but has taken some trouble to use effectively. It would be easy to make a similar commentary upon the whole passage. The new poet might very probably say, "He was as black as bright could be." And the crowd would see how funny it was and the clique would explain how subtle it was. But the clique and the crowd and the poet would all be closer together, if there had been a little more of the subtlety which works through patience to beauty; and the same poet had put the same paradox by saying:

.   .   .   .   .   Darkened so, yet shone
Above them all the Archangel   .   .   .   .   .

No; I am not repeating the common and silly trick of asking Mr. Sitwell why he does not write like Milton; or asking anybody why he does not write like somebody else. Anybody who supposes that I am, is himself deficient in subtlety or, what is more important, in seeing the point. Nobody doubts that the new style, when it is a full and finished style, will be quite different from Milton's style. And what I lament is that it is not

a finished style, because the poet's friends will not leave
the poet alone to finish it. They are so fantastically vain
of having understood it when it was unfinished, that
they rush about boasting of their understanding, that
they may get the glory of it before other people can
understand. It would be far better for the poet if he had
a careless patron or a commonplace public, to whom he
really had to make what is intelligent also intelligible. I
do not mean that he is to make it unintelligent in order
to be intelligible. I shall doubtless be answered by a
fastidious shriek, to the effect that I wish the visionary
to cheapen and vulgarize his vision. I will merely recall
the example I have given, and say that I do certainly
wish an English poem to be written in the vulgar
tongue: like *Paradise Lost*.

The poet, like the priest, should bear the ancient title
of the builder of the bridge. His claim is exactly that
he can really cross the chasm between the world of
unspoken and seemingly unspeakable truths to the
world of spoken words. His triumph is when the bridge
is completed and the word is spoken; above all, when
it is heard. The literary middleman is the man who
always stops the building of the bridge by trying to
meet the builder half-way. A great idea or image grows
in the shadow and often exists long before it is fit for
the daylight. There has been far too much meddling
with the awful obstetrics of art; and too much impor-

tance given to a poem that is unique in the same sense as Macduff. Critics recently expressed a mild surprise that those truly magic casements which Keats saw in his dream had been several times reframed and carpentered before they were open to the public; that the lines exist in manuscript in earlier and inferior forms. The name of Keats has been much invoked by artistic innovators; as if Keats never did anything but innovate. Perhaps those lines, when they were published, were new to the world; but already they were not very new to the poet. If he had simply put down the words, "Peril. Windows. Foaming. Forlorn," he would have written what some modern poets might write and some modern sympathizers might rightly understand. But I think it was well that he went on pegging away until it made some sort of sense; not to mention some sort of melody. And in no spirit of hostility, but rather a real spirit of humility, I do think it would be better if some really original poets of today went on pegging away, until their best effects were more like notes on a musical instrument, and less like notes in a notebook.

For instance, I think that some of Miss Edith Sitwell's casements are really magic casements; but I wish she were allowed to open them a little wider. I wish that some of her effects did not remain select simply by remaining incomplete. She is fond of using the word "unripe" of various things, such as noises and lights; and

the word rather expresses my meaning. I cannot understand, for instance, why a string of images sometimes
as exquisite as jewels should be strung at random on a
metre that may be called, if not a jingle, at any rate
a tinkle. I think it is beautiful poetry to say that:

> The unripe snow tinkles and falls
> Like little tunes on the virginals;

but I still wonder why anybody, who felt an emotion so
worthy of song, should not have put it herself to something a little more like a tune on the virginals and a little
less like a tune on the typewriter. And I cannot help
thinking that if such a genuine poet does this, he will
awaken in a wider human company the ancient instinct
of song. But I do not so much blame the poet, who really
has something to say, as the false and flattering critic
who congratulates the poet on not being able to say it.
He translates him like a distinguished foreigner; he congratulates him merely on being misunderstood: and not
on making himself understood, which is his true function. When Miss Sitwell writes:

> My face is like the King of Spain's map
> All seared with gold; nobody cares a rap.

I do not jeer at it as nonsense; I only regret that many
will recall Mr. Elen and the face that was like a map

of Clapham Junction. I see that there is a fine shade of imagination in the dry and sun-baked brown and gold of Spanish exploration; but I cannot feel that the idea has been brought to its potential perfection of expression. And I grieve most of all over the truest part of the statement. I lament the break-down of the bridge between imagination and understanding; somewhat too sweepingly summed up in the statement that nobody cares a rap.

III. SHAKESPEARE AND SHAW

MANY critics of my own modest writings, as I have had occasion to note elsewhere, have charged me with an excessive love of alliteration. To these it would be apparent that the subject of Shakespeare and Shaw has been created out of the void to satisfy this appetite; whichever of the two surnames I am supposed to have invented or assimilated to the other. Of course there is always the possibility of avoiding it by saying that the works of Shakespeare were written by Bacon; or (what seems to me rather more probable) the works of Shaw written by Sidney Webb. But the truth is, of course, that the two names have been brought together long ago by the deliberate and provocative policy of the bearer of one of them. Shaw has frequently compared himself with Shakespeare; Shakespeare was so unfortunate as to have few opportunities of comparing himself with Shaw. This was perhaps what some of the Shavians have meant by saying that Shakespeare wrote under the disadvantage of his age. This may be, in some respects, true; but it is less universally recognized that Shakespeare wrote under all the advantages of his age and Shaw under all the almost crushing disadvantages of his.

The real truth about this is as much obscured by the
conventional or authoritarian appreciation of Shakespeare as by any pert or juvenile depreciation of Shakespeare; let alone depreciation of Shaw. The view of
those who professed to be most disgusted at the Shavian
impertinence of twenty years ago, the view of those who
constituted themselves the guardians of the sacred Swan
of Avon against the impudent little boy to whom all
swans were geese—this view was in fact equally mistaken about the older and the younger dramatists, about
the poet and about the critic. The swan was none the
less a swan because, having sung its swan-song and died,
it was worshipped largely by geese. But the point is that
the whole conception in both cases was wrong. The conservatives regarded Shakespeare as a sort of earnest and
elevating Modern Thinker, with a Noble Brow; a
hero according to Carlyle and talking in the grand style
as laid down by Matthew Arnold. And that was all
wrong. The same conservatives regarded Bernard Shaw
as a flippant and frivolous mocker of all holy things,
refusing to kiss the pope's toe and preferring to pull the
poet's leg. And that was all wrong. To sum it up in two
pretty adequate parallels; they made the appalling mistake of supposing that Shakespeare was like Goethe and
of supposing that Shaw was like Mephistopheles. But
Shakespeare was not a German, in spite of the unbiassed
conclusion of German scholarship in the matter; he was

the very last man in the world to be cut out for a German hero or a German god. And Shaw is not a devil; far less an imp. The truth is that of the two, it is Shakespeare who is frivolous, or who is at least capable of being irresponsible and gay. It is Shaw, in spite of his real humour, who is much more cut out to be a Goethe, an earnest sage and seer, worshipped by German audiences.

The reason of the greater richness and depth of Shakespeare's gaiety, when he is gay, is in the fact that he came at the end of an epoch of civilization and inherited, however indirectly, all the best of a very ancient culture. The reason for the greater earnestness, or what might even be called the sharper morality, in Shaw and some modern moralists, is that they came after a sort of barbaric interruption that had cut off the countries of the north from Classicism and from Humanism. Goethe was serious, because he had to struggle to recover the lost civilization for the Germans. He had to stretch himself in order to balance and stagger before he could stand upright. But Shakespeare, though he had small Latin and less Greek, had much more in him of the Greek spirit and the Latin order than most of the moderns have ever had; because he received it through a tradition and an atmosphere that had been clear and uninterrupted for some time. For instance, all that light Renaissance pessimism is perfectly incomprehensible to our heavy realistic pessimists. Schopenhauer or Hardy would never be able to understand how cheerfully an Elizabethan said that all roses must fade or that life is brief as a butterfly. Modern sceptics could never understand the subtlety and spiritual complexity with which a Humanist of that age will be talking one moment about Adonis or Apollo, as if they really existed, and the next moment be acknowledging, like Michael Angelo in his last sonnets, that nothing truly exists except Christ upon the Cross. The modern free-thinkers are more simple and in a sense more serious than this. It is they who say that life is real, life is earnest; though curiously enough it is now generally they who go on to say that the grave is certainly its goal.

The Renaissance came late to England; and Shakespeare came late even in the English Renaissance. Only the brilliant accident of a still more belated inheritor, John Milton, makes Shakespeare seem to us to stand somewhere in the middle. But the Humanism, the Hellenism and the pagan mythology mixed with Catholic theology, upon which he fed, had been flowing together from their Italian fountains since the fifteenth century; and long before those great voices of antiquity, the voice of Virgil in poetry and of Aristotle in philosophy, had spoken directly to the whole Christendom of the Middle Ages. Shakespeare was therefore familiar with a mixture of all sorts of moods, memories and fancies, and was not sharply hostile to any of them, save perhaps a little to the Puritans. He could consider a Republican hero of Plutarch, a mediæval king, shining with the sacred chrism as with a nimbus, a pagan misanthrope cursing the world, a Franciscan friar cheerfully and charitably reuniting lovers, a god of the Greek oracles, a goblin of the English country lanes, a fool who was happy or a wise man who was foolish—all without setting one against the other, or thinking there was any particular conflict in the traditions; or asking himself whether he was Classic or Romantic or Mediævalist or Modernist or black or write or buff or blue. Culture was not one strained agony of controversy. That is what I mean by a man inheriting a whole civilization and having the immense advantage of being born three hundred years ago.

By the time that Bernard Shaw was born, the national and religious divisions of Europe had been dug so deep, and had so long sustained what was at once a vigilant rivalry and a fighting in the dark, that this sort of varied and varying balance had become almost impossible. European culture was no longer a many-coloured and stratified thing; it had been split into great fragments by earthquakes. Whatever virtues it might possess, and in a man like Bernard Shaw it does possess some of the most vital of all public virtues, it had produced that curious sort of concentration which did in fact bring forth, first the Shakespearian idolatry by the end of the eighteenth century, and then the Shavian iconoclasm by the end of the nineteenth. Both were not only serious, but entirely serious; in other words, neither was really Shakespearian. Hence arises the paradox upon which I would remark here; that the relations between the idol and the iconoclast are really the very opposite to those which seemed obvious to the idolaters in the days of my youth. It is rather Mr. Bernard Shaw who really has the gravity of the god, or at least of the prophet or oracle of the god; seeing visions of the future and speaking words of the fate of nations. And it is really Shakespeare who passes by in the woods with the elusive laughter of a Faun, and a mystery that has something of mockery.

IV. BERNARD SHAW AND BREAKAGES

As one who has had the honour of conducting a continuous controversy with Mr. Bernard Shaw about everything in earth or heaven, ever since the time of the Boer War, I should like to be allowed to tell him that I think I did see the point of the admirable play called *The Apple Cart;* or rather several points most of the critics have strangely failed to see. I should also like to say that, allowing for the very comparative truth in all such comparisons, I think *The Apple Cart* about the best play he ever wrote.

To take the most trivial matter first, the veteran dramatist is the only dramatist who seems to have any notion of what is really happening in the world today. He has really heard the news of the day; which is much too new to appear in the newspapers. That is why he was accused of senility and fossilized reaction by Mr. Hannen Swaffer, whose onward march of progress seems to have stopped somewhere about the time of the execution of Charles the First. Mr. Swaffer evidently does not know that monarchy is now the mood of the hour everywhere, whether rightly or wrongly; and that popular government is actually less popular than it deserves. I should have every sympathy with Mr. Swaffer if he stood up as a Democrat with the outlook of a Die-hard. I have never been able to understand why this last nickname is always used as a sneer; when it seems rather too heroic a compliment. If an old Radical like myself refused to support those who would die in the last ditch for the mere privilege of landlords or capitalists, it was because of what we thought about the dirtiness of the ditch, not about the doggedness of the dying. And if any other old Radical would own himself old, and even old-fashioned, and die in the Radical ditch, waving a ragged old red flag, I should feel the warmest regard for him; I am not sure that I should not subside into the ditch beside him. But when he has the impudence to accuse a great man of over seventy of being blind with age, because the older man can still see to read the proc-lamations of Mussolini—while the younger is still read-ing the earlier works of Mazzini, I think it is only fair to insist that it is obviously the younger man who is dated and the older man who is up-to-date.

I say this is the most trivial aspect; and I am well aware that it has already worked to the disadvantage of Bernard Shaw's plays; which sometimes seem dated because they were so much up-to-date. A play like *The Philanderer* contains admirable dialogue; but the atmos-phere of the Ibsen Club seems stale, precisely because the boast is not so much that Ibsen is a great topic as that Ibsen is a new topic. In that sense it is always a weakness to boast of being abreast of the times, like Mr. Shaw; but it is worse weakness to boast of being abreast of the times when you are actually behind the times, like Mr. Swaffer. The weakness is in the boasting; and in being primarily concerned about times at all. If Mr. Shaw lives for three hundred years, after the order of Methuselah (as I hope he will) the play of *The Apple Cart* may be as much behind the times as the play of *The Philanderer*. But *Everyman* and *Samson Agonistes* will not be behind the times, but rather beyond time. Anyhow, *The Apple Cart* is not behind the times now, as are nearly all its critics. And there are several examples of this, even more amusing, I think, than the case of the modern reaction to monarchy.

Thus Mr. Shaw mentions one point which I particularly noticed and enjoyed; though many critics, it seems, never noticed it at all. I mean the fact that the Prime Minister's rages, which are so ridiculous considered as rages, are perfectly intelligent and calculated considered as tricks. That is a vital fact of modern government; and nobody has noted it in a play before. The new cunning consists not in hiding the emotions, but in showing the sham emotions. Familiarity is the instrument of falsity; we are no longer deceived by distance or disguise or mystery, but stifled in an embrace and swindled in a heart-to-heart talk. We used to complain that rulers were reverenced as if they were more than human. Our complaint may have been right; but we had not foreseen the filthy and ghastly results of being ruled by those who claim to be human, all too human. We rebelled, and perhaps rightly, when a king was made stiff with gold and gems like an idol, and set on a throne as if it were an altar. We are often tempted today to wish that the new ruler had the good manners of a stone image. We wish he were as well-behaved as a wooden idol or even a wooden-headed king. The king in Mr. Shaw's play is far from wooden-headed; but part of our sympathy with him comes from the vivid vulgarity of the other method, as used by Proteus; who will stoop to pretend weakness in order to preserve power. Politics have never been so frank or so false; we have never before heard so much about the politician's pet-dog and so little about his party fund. Thus the monopolist newspapers, all ruled strictly and secretly by the caprice of one or two millionaires, appear to the public eye as one vast sea of slush and sob-stuff, of people weeping over what they never suffered or confessing what they never did. Emotional expediency, the method of Mr. Proteus, is now familiar to many people; but not to many dramatists or dramatic critics.

But my real reason for submitting this comment on Mr. Shaw's communication is concerned with a third example; in which he is especially abreast of the crisis and ahead of the critics. Hardly anybody has really understood the point about Breakages, Ltd.; because nearly everybody is about six stages behind in the actual development of individualism into industrialism. Mr. Shaw is exactly on the very last lap or turn of intelligent criticism. First, of course, there was the time when Capitalism boasted of competition, and dreaded a Trust as much as a Trade Union. The hard-headed Manchester man of this period still lingers on the stage, along with the comic curate and the French maid. Then came the time when Capitalism crushed competition; for it was Capitalism and not Socialism that crushed it. Those who had denounced Trusts were told to defend Trusts; and they did so, hurriedly explaining that monopoly is the same as efficiency, that amalgamation is the fashion and must be followed, and that the individual trader is a relic of the past. So we let ourselves be completely conquered by Trusts; an appropriate title, for it was a touching manifestation of Trust. When Trusts were finally established, they began for the first time to be seriously considered. And then the fun began. It is as yet only fun for a few; but among the few are Mr. Shaw and, if I may so, myself. To some of us at least it is more and more obvious that there is not a word of truth in the eulogy on the Capitalist Trust; even in the muddy materialistic eulogy that its flatterers give it. It has not only destroyed the virtues it despises; such as independence, individuality and liberty. It has also destroyed the very

virtues that it claims; efficiency and modernity and practical progress. Big Business is not business-like; it is not
enterprising; it is not favourable to science and invention. By the very nature of its monopoly of machinery
and mass production, it works entirely the other way.
Millions are sunk in plants that cannot be changed or
brought up-to-date. Machinery is made so that it must
be used, even when it is useless. Things are made badly
so that they must be mended. Things are even made
badly so that they may be mended badly; and therefore
mended again. Under the beneficent influence of the
Merger, we are actually ruled by Inefficiency; not by
individual or accidental Inefficiency, but by sustained
and systematic Inefficiency; by the principle of Inefficiency; by the sacred rule and religion of Inefficiency.
In other words, as the dramatist notes, we are ruled by
Breakages, Ltd.

Lastly, few seem to have realized that the play is a
tragedy; that it does not turn on the comedy of the conversation between the American Ambassador and the
King, but on the tragedy of the absence of any conversation between the American Ambassador and the Cabinet.
Compared with the Cabinet squabbles, the visit of the
American Ambassador to the English Court is like the
visit of a vast comet to the earth. And it is implied that
the Cabinet is quite capable of continuing to squabble,
even if a comet did visit the earth. Those who worship

the colossal, whether in comets or commerce, might possibly even rejoice that England was merged in America, or rejoice (for all I know) that the earth was merged in the senseless star-dust of a larger luminary. But men of imagination never worship the colossal. King Magnus is made a man of imagination; he is made a subtle and attractive personality; he is made sympathetic in fact, for the very simple reason that he is the hero of a tragedy. There is exactly the same type of attractiveness deliberately attributed to Hamlet or to Othello. For great tragedy is only great when it describes loss so as to increase value, and not to decrease it.

V. THE POPULARITY OF DICKENS

THE last attempt to treat a Victorian hero as a whited sepulchre, and create a sensation by scraping off the whitewash, failed in a special degree for a special reason. It failed, not only because the whiteness was not merely whitewash, but even more because it was not enough of a sepulchre. Dickens was not exactly what is implied, either among the iconoclasts or the idolaters, by a Victorian hero. He was not even really Victorian, let alone heroic. He did not really belong to that world of seriousness which some call Victorian, when they mean rather Tennysonian. He had no more real respect for what Mrs. Garvin has aptly called "the blue-blood of the brain" than he had for any other sort of blue-blood. What he really represented was red blood; and he got it from Smollett and Fielding and men who lived before the delicate compromise of Victorian virtue was known. It is too often forgotten that the most Dickensian of Dickens's works was not Victorian at all. The Queen was barely crowned when Pickwick was filling the land with laughter over the descriptions of a pre-Victorian social life. It was long afterwards that Carlyle began to fill the land with the solemn litanies of Hero-Worship; and the entirely new and rather German notion of taking men of genius seriously. This idea of gravity about great men did not greatly possess the drinking and dicing England of the eighteenth century; and it did not possess Dickens at all. He had not even enough hero-worship; and his prospects in life did not particularly encourage him to be a hero. But the point to seize is that the atmosphere of the beginning of the nineteenth century in England was rather an atmosphere of the grotesque and a jolly ugliness. It was the end of the nineteenth century that has left us, for good and evil, with the memory of a Tennysonian prettiness. "Her court was pure, her life serene" does not exhaust the ways in which the first volumes of *Punch* talked about the Court. Indeed the very figure of Punch is typical of the change. There is something pathetic in the efforts of the last Victorian artists to irradiate the face of Mr. Punch with the most pious and idealistic emotions. But men who had set out intending to express all the ideals of the "Idylls of the King" would never have chosen a figure like Mr. Punch at all.

Now the first thing to realize about the maker of Pickwick is that he originally breathed the same air as the makers of Punch. While he rose in the social scale and took on some of the mid-Victorian conventions, and generally gained a sober colouring from a world that was being toned down by the high-toned Ruskin and the rest, there remained in him something that was never quite serious, any more than one of his favourite show-

men or cheapjacks was quite serious. He had any
amount of anger and vanity; he boasted and picked quarrels as cheapjacks do; but he did not really see himself
in a prophet's mantle as Carlyle and Ruskin and Tenny-
son did. It is characteristic that tradition would vaguely
imagine the other three men as tall; but we do not
think of Dickens as tall, though he was not abnormally
short. We think of him as a vivacious little figure, making everybody laugh, chiefly with him but occasionally
at him. He was Sam Weller; he was the English poor
man, whose weapon is humour. He was always in a
sense the comic servant mocking the solemn master, like
Sancho Panza following Don Quixote. And the serious
charges against him have failed; not only for the simple
reason that they were false; but also for the more subtle
reason, that they were serious. You cannot tear the mask
off Dick Swiveller; it is like trying to tear the wig off
Mr. Micawber and finding he does not wear one.

For this reason, as well as many others, I think that
Dickens's popularity is secure; if we ever reach conditions in which there can be a true popularity, unaffected
by what is called publicity and ought to be called plutocracy. There is no real test, in an American atmosphere
where the best-seller is only a tribute to the best salesman. But if ever we recover anything like a human quiet
in which people can hear themselves think, I have no
doubt that they will think it more fun to read Dickens

than to read Dreiser. It is said that many have no patience
to read Dickens; it would be truer to say that they have
no time to read Dickens; their time being occupied with
wasting their time on things they do not really want to
read. But if we ever see again the psychological miracle
of liberty (that is of men wanting anything) I have no
doubt that masses will still want Dickens; and many who
never really knew what they wanted. In some respects,
indeed, Dickens does not suffer from being too old a
writer, but from being too new a writer. In many ways
he was singularly free from the illusions of his time;
much more free than a good many people in our time.
He did not imagine, as so many men much better educated did imagine, that Parliament was a pattern to the
whole world. He has left on record words that might
have been written by a Fascist or Syndicalist in the twentieth century rather than a respectable Radical in the
nineteenth. Much of his satire can be best understood
in relation to much more recent satirists, who have been
accused of exaggeration by much more recent critics.
Mr. Veneering's Election had its immediate sequel in
Mr. Clutterbuck's Election; and anyone who will read
Little Dorrit and the description of the great affiliated
families of Barnacle and Stiltstalking will know that
Dickens discovered forty years before what Mr. Belloc
discovered forty years afterwards. Only many critics
have not discovered it even now. But the point is impor-

tant touching popularity. Dickens will not suffer with
the change of costumes. He will gain by the decay of
disguises. Thackeray thought just a little too much of
Major Pendennis because he was then in the height of
fashion. Dickens did not care a button about Major
Bagstock; and it will not matter whether he is old-
fashioned. This potential victory over time comes from
the same popular root of popularity. Sam Weller may
have grown more decorous as Mr. Pickwick grew more
grave; but Sam is still Sam; he is still making fun of
everything, including Mr. Pickwick. He was not born
a butler, like the solemn servants of the Merdles or the
Veneerings. It is not for nothing that he ran wild in the
streets and was a waggoner's boy and a carter's boy, before he ever put on livery. So there was something in
Dickens that had run wild with the old coarse and
candid and popular satire of the past. "He could not
describe a gentleman"; which means that he could never
quite keep a straight face while describing one. He served
the ideals of his generation, or all that was best in them,
with brilliant courage and zeal: humanity and liberty
and tenderness to the fallen and hope for all. But he
never really served the idols of his generation, or he could
never serve them without smiling; he was outside the
clubs and the cliques and the constitutional movements.
That is what was meant by calling him a caricaturist. To
him these things were still strange things, like monsters.

He had his weaknesses, though they were small beside his enthusiasm and his pity; but he was curiously without a weakness of much stronger men; he was not really deceived by the pomps and vanities of this wicked world.

VI. MAGIC AND FANTASY IN FICTION

IT may seem but a mild form of dalliance to trifle with the word Magic as a term of criticism, when it has recently been so useful to the clergy as a term of abuse. We know that Dr. Barnes of Birmingham has shown all the ancient activity of a witch-smeller, in pursuing those suspected of believing it, as the witch-smellers pursued those suspected of practising it. He does this, I understand, to show that he is a Liberal Churchman. I have no intention of discussing such matters here; but it does happen that this use of the term, considered as a text, throws some light on the first facts of its relation to literature, and especially to legend. The ecclesiastic in question always uses it as covering all the rather wide field of religious doctrines in which he does not happen to believe. But in this we have at the start the neglect of an important and rather interesting distinction. The word Magic was widely used as a term of abuse, because it was really a question of abuse in more senses than one. Magic was the abuse of preternatural powers, by lower agents whose work was preternatural but not supernatural. It was founded on the profound maxim of *diabolus simius Dei;* the devil is the ape of God. Magic was a monkey trick of imitation of the divine functions;

and there was therefore nothing strange in either the similarity or the dissimilarity. But to talk of the higher mysteries or miracles as forms of magic, or as coming forth from magic, is to reverse the whole story. It is as if we were to say that the Black Mass gradually evolved into the Mass. It is like saying that an Abbot establishing the rule of St. Benedict was a parody of the Abbot of Misrule. It is like saying that the disciples who said the Lord's Prayer had borrowed it from the witches who said it backwards.

But in all that mythology and popular poetry, out of which our written literature sprang, this distinction is dimly felt long before it was clarified by Christianity. There is always the sense of one sort of magic which is an enemy and an enslaver. We all know that there are jokes of philology, or examples in which a word has been turned upside down and come to mean the contrary of itself. The learned will readily grow gay over the history of the word "buxom," or the word "nervous." There is almost as comic a contradiction in our use of the word "enchantment" when we say "I was enchanted to meet Mr. Miggs," or "The view of Brixton from the station is simply enchanting." But in the vast unwritten literature of mankind enchantment was almost always regarded as a curse. There is in enchantment almost always an idea of captivity. Sometimes the stricken victim is literally struck motionless, as when men are turned

to stone by the Gorgon, or the prince in the Arabian
Tale is clamped to the earth in marble. Quite as often
the victim of enchantment wanders through the woods
as a white hind, or flies with apparent freedom as a par-
rot or a wild swan. But he always talks of his very freedom as a wandering imprisonment. And the reason is
that there is always in such witchcraft the note of trav-
esty; the man is disguised and in a double sense
"guyed"; as when the youth in Apuleius feels literally
that the witches have made an ass of him. In contrast
with this, it will be noted that the good miracles, the acts
of the saints and heroes, are always acts of restoration.
They give the victim back his personality; and it is a
normal and not a super-normal personality. The miracle gives back his legs to the lame man; but it does not
turn him into a large centipede. It gives eyes to the
blind; but only a regular and respectable number of eyes.
The paralytic is told to stretch forth his hand, which is
the gesture of liberation from fetters; but not to spread
himself as a sort of Briarean octopus radiating in all di-
rections and losing the human form. There runs through
the whole tradition the idea that black magic is that
which blots out or disguises the true form of a thing;
while white magic, in the good sense, restores it to its
own form and not another. St. Nicholas brings two
children alive out of a pot when they have already been
boiled down into soup; which may be said to mark the

extreme assertion of form against formlessness. But Medea, being a witch, puts an old man into a pot and promises to bring out a young man; that is, another man. Also Medea, being a witch, does not keep her word.

This division, even in the deep roots of legend and primitive literature, would help critics very much in judging the real principles of uncanny or fantastic fiction. There is no reason within reason, why literature should not describe the demonic as well as the divine aspect of mystery or myth. What is really remarkable is that in modern fiction, in an age accused of frivolity, in an age perhaps only too headlong in its pursuit of happiness, or at least of hedonism, the only popular sort of fantasy is the unhappy fantasy. There is a certain amount of fantasy that is avowedly fantastic, in the sense of unreal; mostly in the form of fairy-tales ostensibly written for children. But, on the whole, when the serious modern novel has dealt with the serious preternatural agency, it has not only been serious but sad. This contrast appears first and most vividly in the comfortable and even convivial Victorian novelists. They often thought it enough to make their human characters comfortable; but if they did suggest any superhuman characters, they were generally uncomfortable as well as uncanny. These humanitarians of the nineteenth century were haunted by no spirits, except a few thin

ghosts; but these were the lost spirits of Calvinists of
the seventeenth century. In their philosophies, the
humanitarians believed in heaven but not in hell. In
their novels, they believed in hell but not in heaven.
Dickens did indeed attempt in the *Christmas Carol* to
make a positive polytheism of three versions of Father
Christmas; a curious temporal Trinity. But the warmest
Dickensian (and I hope I am one of the warmest) will
admit that these solid guides are far less convincing than
the visions that they reveal. They have not that purely
poetic reality that does belong to the hints of horror and
the glimpses of nightmare in the novels of Dickens.
The man with the waxen face, in one of his short stories,
is by every definition a ghost; but he is a ghost in whom
we can believe, as compared with these gods in whom we
cannot believe. It was even more marked in Wilkie Collins, who had less sense of the serious need of spiritual
things. He could indulge himself in dubious superstition; he would have thought it superstitious to indulge in
the symbols of positive religion. The whole point of
Armadale is a family curse as frankly psychic as a family
ghost. But we should be much disconcerted, in wandering through a Wilkie Collins story, to meet an angel
with wings and a halo when we were looking for a
gentleman with whiskers and a high hat.

In short, in so far as humanity became once more
heathen, it believed more and more in the old dehu-

manizing spell, the freezing of the will by trance or terror, and less in the other legend of the hero or the helper who can break the spell. There has lately been a return to the more heartening heroic legend; but that is exactly in so far as there has been a reaction against the merely heathen spirit. A story like *The Bridge of San Luis Rey* is strictly supernatural and not merely preternatural. But even here the habit of the nineteenth century persists into the twentieth, especially in the instinctive selection of form. No man has done more to bring back a breath of happiness into fantasy than Mr. Walter de la Mare. He has testified that even when we do look through magic casements, it is not absolutely necessary that the faerie lands should be forlorn. But, by something almost like a sense of delicacy, he has generally brought his good news in the form of rhymes; and in a sense merely of nursery rhymes. It gives a note, not exactly of irresponsibility, but of a certain shyness and appeal to innocence. But when it is a matter of more massive treatment, even he inherits something of the now established "modern" spirit, which can deal most decisively with the darker experience. And few things that he, or indeed anybody else, has written have so much of what can really be called realism as the diabolism of "Seaton's Aunt."

It is perhaps a symbol that Henry James called one of his books "The Two Magics"; but entirely forgot to

mention any magic except one. For in the other case
the word is a mere metaphor, used of some trick or tact;
and the only tale that is really about magic is about
black magic. It was a horrible and powerful story about
two children practically possessed of devils. I wish somebody with the genius of James could really write a book
on "The Two Magics"; and say something in the other
of the gesture that can cast out devils. As it is, even the
most sensitive and spiritual modern fiction leaves us
rather with the Swinburnian impression that "even He
who cast seven devils out of Magdalene" could scarcely
do the same for Seaton's aunt. I am well aware that there
has been an interlude of a rather different sort of magic,
which professed for a time to be neither black nor white.
If I call it colourless magic, I do not mean it in contempt;
but rather as crystals are colourless, or diamonds or clear
water. It came with what was called the Celtic School
when Victorian ethics, always rather exhausting, were
rather exhausted. In that reaction it was rational enough
for Mr. W. B. Yeats to bid us "Come clear of the nets
of wrong and of right"; and so ignore even the two
kinds of positive magic, the net of St. Peter and the
snare of Satan. But I, who have an inexhaustible admiration for everything that Mr. Yeats says and writes, may
be allowed to testify that any attempt to live entirely in
the crystal of colourless magic ends in the very convincing exclamation of the elf in his own play, "I am tired

of winds and waters and pale lights." So were we; and so eventually was Mr. Yeats; for his powerful mind seems to have turned more and more of late to structural visions of the whole course of history and humanity; social and rather sweeping statements like intellectual cyclones, which must nevertheless in their nature be not only mystical but moral. And though I do not care very much myself for the cabalistic games and cryptograms that seem to amuse him at present, they have a certain mathematical solidity like Babylonian bricks. It is a good thing in that sense to be a Cubist, when winds and water have tempted you too much to be a Curvist. But in any case I am convinced that every deep or delicate treatment of the magical theme, from the lightest jingle of Peacock Pie, which may seem as nonsensical as Lear, to the most profound shaking of the phenomenal world, as in some of the best stories of Algernon Blackwood, will always be found to imply an indirect relation to the ancient blessing and cursing; and it is almost as vital that it should be moral as that it should not be moralizing. Magic for magic's sake, like art for art's sake, is found in fact to be too shallow, and to be unable to live without drawing upon things deeper than itself. To say that all real art is in black and white is but another way of saying that it is in light and darkness; and there is no fantasy so irresponsible as really to escape from the alternative.

After all, it is perhaps no matter of surprise that Bishop Barnes of Birmingham should see a link between the Magician and the Mass. There is a sort of logical link between them; the logical link that connects Yes and No. In other words, they are exact contraries; like light and darkness, which are often classed together because they are often mentioned at once. They cross each other with the complete collision and contradiction that belongs to "The Two Magics." The Magician is the Man when he seeks to become a God, and, being a usurper, can hardly fail to be a tyrant. Not being the maker, but only the distorter, he twists all things out of their intended shape, and imprisons natural things in unnatural forms. But the Mass is exactly the opposite of a Man seeking to be a God. It is a God seeking to be a Man; it is God giving his creative life to mankind as such, and restoring the original pattern of their manhood; making not gods, nor beasts, nor angels; but, by the original blast and miracle that makes all things new, turning men into men.

THE END